W9-ARP-873

CLASSIC

MAGIC
TRICKS

CLASSIC

MAGIC TRICKS

Bob Longe, David Knowles,
and Charles Barry Townsend

Main Street
A division of Sterling Publishing Co., Inc.
New York

Material in this collection was adapted from

World's Best Coin Tricks © 1992 by Bob Longe
Easy Magic Tricks © 1994 by Bob Longe
World's Best Magic Tricks © 1992 by Charles Barry Townsend
Spooky Magic Tricks © 1993 by David Knowles
Spine-Tingling Magic Tricks © 2001 by Sterling Publishing Company

10 9 8 7 6 5 4 3

© 2002 by Sterling Publishing Co., Inc.
Published by Sterling Publishing Co., Inc.
387 Park Avenue South, New York, NY 10016
Distributed in Canada by Sterling Publishing
c/o Canadian Manda Group, One Atlantic Avenue, Suite 105
Toronto, Ontario, Canada M6K 3E7
Distributed in Great Britain by Chrysalis Books Group PLC
The Chrysalis Building, Bramley Road, London W10 6SP, England
Distributed in Australia by Capricorn Link (Australia) Pty. Ltd.
P.O. Box 704, Windsor, NSW 2756, Australia

Printed in China
All rights reserved

Sterling ISBN 1-4027-1070-4

CONTENTS

INTRODUCTION

Probably the first trick anyone bought from the display wall of a magic shop lured them with the claim, "no skill required." If you believed that claim, you probably found out you were fooling yourself. Magic is a skill. Even the simplest self-working trick takes skill to perform. And the only way to get this kind of magical skill is by practice, but it really isn't as bad as it seems. Practicing magic is not only fun, it's rewarding as well.

You may also have heard the phrase, "magic is all done with mirrors." In a sense, this is true because the best way to practice magic tricks is in front of a mirror. When you practice in a mirror, you see tricks just as the audience will see them. That makes it a lot easier to learn to perform the moves smoothly, stand in the right position and hold the props at the proper angles so that you don't accidentally expose the secrets of the tricks.

Practicing in front of a mirror will also give you a sense of timing. Pacing is as important to a magician as it is to a comedian. A successful, well-executed, well-timed trick is like a story. It has a beginning, a middle, and an end. You have to pace each trick so there is a buildup of mystery. If you rush through it, the mystery will be lost. If, on the other hand, you drag a trick out too long, spectators could lose interest.

The magic tricks you'll find in this book not only fool, they're also interesting, surprising, amusing—in a word, entertaining. The majority can be performed with everyday objects: cards, coins, string, rubber bands, safety pins, handkerchiefs, dice, and—always at hand, of course—your own fingers. Some tricks require props or gimmicks that can be constructed easily.

To help you achieve maximum impact, you'll be taught precisely how to perform each trick, including hints on patter.

TIPS

When You've Goofed: We're all familiar with the person who has an excuse for everything. *Nothing* is ever that person's fault. When a trick doesn't go right, you can recover and create amusement by pretending to be that person.

You might make such feeble excuses as:

"Of course that's the wrong card. I did that just to test you."

"So the string still has a knot in it. I did that on purpose. It's a joke. Ha-ha-ha-ha."

Or, the minute someone calls your attention to a mistake, instantly and very rapidly say, "I knew that." Then fill in with whatever preposterous excuse occurs to you.

The Joke's on You: Avoid making a fool of the spectator who assists you. Yes, the joke may be on him or her, but your manner should be kindly. If possible, share the role of victim with them. *Both* of you are astonished at the turn of events. Even better, make the joke turn on yourself as often as you can.

The Audience Is Your Friend: Please remember that you and the audience are sharing an experience. Together you're fooled, shocked, amazed, amused. You're just as surprised as everyone else. The audience (of whatever size) should like not only the tricks, they should also like *you.*

MIND READING MAGIC

MATH WIZARDRY

A Quick Math Mystery

Effect: In passing, remark that you were born with an uncanny mathematical talent. For some reason, you are able merely to look at a number and tell if the number can be evenly divided by 4, no matter how many digits it contains. And if the number cannot be evenly divided by 4, you can figure out how to make it evenly divisible by adding one or two digits to it.

To illustrate your talent, invite someone to write down a random number of up to 20 digits. Let's assume he writes down the number 284502958123291044392. Glance at the number for a second or two and declare that it cannot be evenly divided by 4, but that you'll fix it so that it can be. Then add the number 28 to the end of the number and instruct the person who wrote down the number to try dividing it by 4. Sure enough, after a minute of hard work, he will find that the number 28450295812329104439228 can indeed be evenly divided by 4. Chalk another one up for the Mental Wizard.

Presentation: The answer to this mystery is almost too simple. The truth is that any number that you add 28 to can be evenly divided by 4. A long number, with over 15 digits, helps to throw the spectators off the track. This trick is very effective, but don't repeat it or the method becomes obvious. Use the trick as an effective filler between two other larger, and more complicated, mental mysteries. Present it as a sort of afterthought, an interesting aside into the many avenues of your mental powers.

Magic Memory

Here's a mental mystery that will astound your friends. Make several photocopies of the card shown in *Illus. A1* and mount them on fairly stiff cardboard. When you present this trick, pass the cards out and request that members of the audience call out any of the two-digit numbers enclosed in parentheses. Immediately tell them what the seven-digit number below it is. You can do the whole card if they can stand it. The secret of your amazing memory is very simple; it goes like this:

A) Take the number they give you, say 25, and add 11 to it (giving us 36 for this example).
B) Reverse the result. This gives you the first two digits of your answer (63).
C) From this point on, always add the previous two numbers as you construct your number. The third digit will be 9.
D) For the fourth digit, add 3 and 9, getting 12. When the sum gives you a double-digit answer, drop the 10's position and use the unit's position. Our digit here is 2.

E) The fifth digit is 1 (9 plus 2 = 11, drop the 10's position, and use the unit's position 1).

F) The sixth digit is 3 (2 plus 1 = 3).

G) The seventh and final digit is 4 (1 plus 3 = 4).

Our final answer for the number 25 is 6392134.

With a little practice, you should be able to do all of these calculations in your head. When you're giving the answers, it's best to have a blackboard or large pad to write on so that your audience can see the number as you "recall" it. Also, writing down the number on a blackboard makes it easier for you to mentally generate it.

Now go forth and mystify the world, O Mighty Master of Mathematical Marvels and Miscellaneous Meanderings.

(23)	(39)	(18)	(22)	(4)	(38)
4370774	0550550	9213471	3369549	5167303	9437077
(2)	(45)	(30)	(34)	(25)	(6)
3145943	6516730	1459437	5493257	6392134	7189763
(9)	(37)	(46)	(3)	(1)	(17)
0224606	8426842	7527965	4156178	2134718	8202246
(21)	(5)	(44)	(11)	(41)	(19)
2358314	6178538	5505505	2246066	2572910	0336954
(29)	(12)	(33)	(13)	(43)	(7)
0448202	3257291	4482022	4268426	4594370	8190998

Illus. A1

Lightning Addition

Effect: In this mental masterpiece, you will show your audience that you can add up a column of numbers before it's even written down. Get someone from the audience to help you with this one. On a large blackboard or drawing pad, write down the number 234. Have your assistant write any three-digit number under it. Now write a three-digit number under his. Continue doing this three more times, at which point he will have written down four numbers and you will have written five. Now draw a line under the column and have him add the numbers up. He'll come up with the number 4,230. Point to an envelope on your table and tell him to open it. Inside he'll find a sheet of paper with, "The total of the numbers will be 4,230" written on it.

Materials Needed:
- An envelope with the total written down on a piece of paper inside
- A large blackboard or drawing pad

Presentation: Obviously, you are going to control the column of numbers so that the final total will be 4,230. The first number that you wrote down was your key number. The next eight numbers were written down in a series of four pairs; first the assistant wrote a number and then you wrote another number under it. Every number you wrote under the one he had written will, when added to his, give you a total of 999. Here's an example of how it would look:

(1)	234
(2)	321
(3)	678
(4)	972
(5)	027
(6)	321
(7)	678
(8)	422
(9)	577
Total	4,230

You'll notice that the pairs of numbers 2–3, 6–7, and 8–9 each total 999. In other words, when he wrote down 321 you wrote 678 under it. Added together, they total 999.

If you were to take the key number that you wrote first, 234, and subtract 4 from it, you would get the last three numbers of the total. Also, if you then took that 4 and placed it in front of the number, you would then have 4,230, the total. The reason that we subtract 4 from the key number is that 4 represents the number of paired numbers we wrote under the key number.

Knowing how the key number works allows you to repeat the trick using a different key number, thus giving you a different total every time.

EXCITING ESP

A Mental Card Mystery

Effect: Instruct a spectator to sit down at the table, and hand him a stack of nine cards. Say, "Here are nine cards from the deck, ace through nine. I want you to shuffle these cards, and when you're through, please deal them into three rows of three cards each (as in *Illus. A2*). While you're doing this, I'm going to be seated over here with my back toward you."

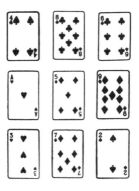

Illus. A2

When the participant has finished dealing out the cards, tell him to remove any one of the cards, show it to the audience, and then place it in his pocket. When this is done, he is to add up the three rows of numbers represented by the cards. He is to consider the empty space from the card that he pocketed as a zero. In the example shown in *Illus. A3*, the total comes to 1,008.

Finally, the participant is instructed to add up all of the figures in the answer and to tell the performer what their sum is. In our example, the sum would be 9. The magician now, without turning around, states that the card that the spectator has chosen and pocketed is the 9 of diamonds. This is, of course, the right answer.

Illus. A3

Materials Needed:
• One deck of cards

Presentation: This trick works every time. You can have the spectator replace the card that he chose, rearrange the cards, and do it again and you will have no trouble in telling him what his new card is. All that you have to do is to take the number that he gives you and subtract it from 9 to get the value of the card. If the number is greater than 8, as in our example, simply subtract the number from 18 to get the card number. The suit of the card is calculated as follows.

1. The red cards are always odd, the black cards are always even.
2. Numerically, the first two odd cards (ace and 3) are hearts.
3. Numerically, the next three odd cards (5, 7, 9) are diamonds.
4. Numerically, the first two even cards (2 and 4) are spades.
5. Numerically, the next two even cards (6 and 8) are clubs.

With a little practice, you should have this trick down pat in no time.

X-ray Vision

Effect: In this trick, you, the magician or mentalist, work openly with an assistant. Claim that your assistant has the powers of a true medium and can perform many wondrous feats, such as predicting the future, turning lead to gold, and actually being able to see through solid walls and other impenetrable objects. Tonight the two of you are going to give a small demonstration of this great power.

Ask the medium to leave the room with a member of the audience, to keep him under surveillance. Once they are out of the room, request the help of someone else from the audience. Instruct this person to take your deck of cards, shuffle it, and freely select any card in front of the rest of the audience. Then hand the spectator a sheet of aluminum foil and request that he wrap the card in it so that no portion of the card is visible. Next, give him an envelope and tell him to seal the card inside and to place the envelope in his coat pocket and wait for the medium to return.

Now state that you will leave the room before the medium is brought back to demonstrate his abilities. When the medium returns, he should stop and stare at the spectator with the envelope for several seconds, and then name the card.

Materials Needed:
- One deck of cards
- Roll of aluminum foil in its box
- An envelope

Presentation: Since you are not in the room when the medium returns, you must leave something there that will indicate to the medium what card the spectator has selected. It has to be something that will not arouse any suspicion among the audience. What you use is the box of aluminum foil on the table. As soon as the card is selected, you and the rest of the audience will know its identity. After you tear off a piece of foil to wrap the card in, place the foil box back on the table. Where, and how, you place it will signal to the medium the identity of the chosen card.

The table is mentally divided into twelve sections, each section representing a card value ranging from ace (as the lowest card) to queen *(Illus. A4)*. Placing the box in any one of these sections will indicate its value. Placing the box anywhere on the table with any part of it sticking over the edge of the table will indicate that the card is a king.

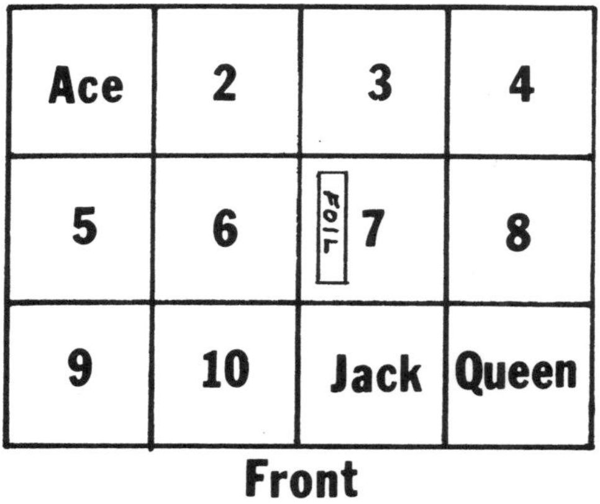

Ace	2	3	4
5	6	7	8
9	10	Jack	Queen

Front

Illus. A4

The way you place the box on the table will indicate to the medium the *suit* of the card *(Illus. A5)*. If the box is perpendicular to the front edge of the table and the flap is to the right, then the suit is spades. If the flap is to the left, then the suit is clubs. If the box is parallel to the front edge of the table and the flap is to the front, then the suit is hearts. If the flap is to the back, then the suit is diamonds.

The beauty of using the box to convey the card's identity is the fact that it is on the table during your whole act. You only handle it briefly, and it supposedly has no relation to the trick being performed. With the right presentation, this can be a stellar effect in your act.

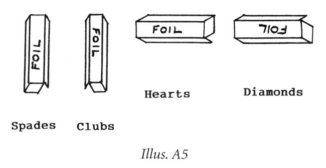

Hearts   Diamonds

Spades   Clubs

Illus. A5

A Thought-Transference Trick

Effect: Tell the audience that you and your assistant will perform an experiment concerning Second Sight. Tell your assistant to sit on a chair in a corner of the room facing the wall, and then ask someone from the audience to blindfold your assistant, walk around the room, and touch an object. Let's say he touches a vase. Ask your blindfolded assistant, "Did he touch the lamp? The piano? The chair? The rug? The vase?" At this point, the assistant replies, "Yes, it was the vase that was touched!"

You and your assistant should continue in this manner identifying five or six more objects touched by members of the audience. Never change the tone of your voice or make any other noise that could possibly convey a message to your blindfolded assistant. Is this truly a case of Second Sight?

Presentation: No, it's Second Sight, but only the use of a clever prearranged code. Before the performance, get together with your assistant and work out the following verbal code: Agree that the object touched will be the second one you mention after you name an object that starts with the letter C. In the example just given, the first C object that you, the magician, asked about was a chair. Two objects later, you mentioned the vase.

You and your assistant should agree on a set of key letters to be used. This way, when you repeat the trick, begin the key word with a different letter each time, to throw off the audience. A little practice beforehand will ensure a successful performance and should leave your audience wondering how in the world you did it.

Mind Under Matter

George Sanders discovered the principle; Martin Gardner invented the trick.

Grace seems to take ESP quite seriously. She's the perfect subject for this trick. Explain, "I'd like to check your ESP, Grace." Hand her a deck of cards. "Would you please remove the queen of spades and six other cards? As you know, the queen of spades is supposed to have mysterious powers, so I'd like to see how long it takes you to find her."

When she removes the seven cards, she'll probably have them face up on the table. Pick them up with the queen of spades at the face of the packet. Turn the packet over. In a series of casual overhand shuffles, move the queen to the top, then to the bottom, and then back to the top.

"Grace, I'd like you to choose a number from one to six." Suppose she names four. Hand her the packet. "Now I'd like you to move four cards from the top to the bottom, one at a time. Then turn over the next card." She does so. "No, it's not the queen of spades. Try again." Beginning with the face-up card, she again moves four from the top to the bottom of the packet and turns up the next card. Wrong again. In fact, she turns over six wrong cards in a row. At this point, you take the packet from her and fan through, showing that there's only one face-down card. Pull out the queen of spades and show it. "Wonderful, Grace! You have strong negative ESP." Place the queen of spades on the bottom and repeat the shuffling procedure, ending with the queen on top. Hand her the packet again.

"Try it again, Grace. Choose a different number." Once more the queen of spades is the last face-down card.

Perhaps one or two others would like to check out their ESP. They, too, will fail. The stunt can be repeated indefinitely, but three or four times should provide sufficient amusement.

A Mental Magic Square

Effect: Stand in front of the audience and say: "Magic Squares rank as one of the oldest mental amusements in history. In the past it took mathematicians days or even weeks to construct specific squares. In this age of computers it can be done somewhat more quickly, but I have found that given the right training the human mind can do as well. To prove this point I am going to attempt to construct, in my head, a magic square composed of 16 different numbers. Madam, will you give me a number between three and ten? Four will be fine. And you, sir, could I have a number between zero and ten? Seven, very good! I will now generate a magic square for you that will add up to 47 in each horizontal row, in each vertical column, and in each of the major diagonal lines. Quiet, please!

"Yes, I can see the answer now. The numbers are falling into place. I will now fill in the grid on this drawing pad with the finished magic square.

"There it is folks, and I've added a bonus! The four corner squares on each side, plus the four center squares, also add up to 47. That was exhausting. Please keep this drawing as a souvenir."

That's your presentation. Now we'll tell you how it's done.

Materials Needed:
- An easel
- A large newsprint sketching pad
- A large-tip black marking pen
- A light-blue pencil
- A ruler

Preparation: Take the pad and draw on it a large sixteen-square grid with your black marking pen and a ruler. At the top of the pad where you have folded over the cover of the pad, write the following four sets of numbers lightly with the blue pencil: (7, 10, 13+) (12+, 1, 6, 11) (2, 15+, 8, 5) (9, 4, 3, 14+). They should be written small so that they can only be seen up close by you and not by anyone sitting in the audience. These figures are there to prompt you in case you forget any of them when you're writing down the magic square.

Presentation: The key to creating this type of Magic Square is knowing a secret mathematical formula. *Illus. A6* shows how the magic square for the number 47 was generated. (Remember that you can create a magic square with any number greater than 40. However, it's suggested that you use a two-figure number.) Start with the number 47. Subtract 30 from it, and then divide the difference (17) by 4. This will leave you with a dividend of 4 and a remainder of 1.

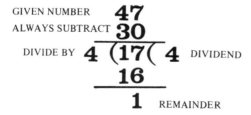

THE SECRET MATHEMATICAL FORMULA

GIVEN NUMBER **47**
ALWAYS SUBTRACT **30**
DIVIDE BY **4 (17(4** DIVIDEND
16
1 REMAINDER

Illus. A6

Next, look at *Illus. A7*. In each one of the squares (except square *D*), you will find a number in a circle. This is the initial value of the square. You must add the dividend (4) to this value to get the final value for the square. For square *D*, enter only the value of the dividend (4). In the four games that have a plus sign (+) next to the circled initial amount (squares *C, E, J, P*), also add the remainder (1) from your calculation to get the final value for the square.

A	B	C	D
⑦	⑩	⑬ +	
E	F	G	H
⑫ +	①	⑥	⑪
I	J	K	L
②	⑮ +	⑧	⑤
M	N	O	P
⑨	④	③	⑭ +

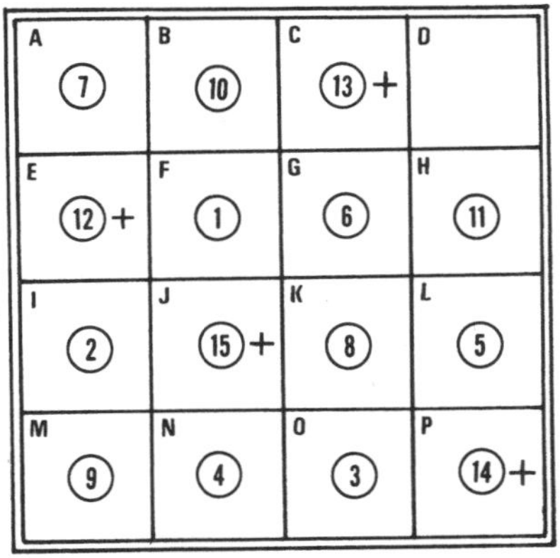

Illus. A7

Our sample square would thus be created as follows: (A) 7 + 4 = 11; (B) 10 + 4 = 14; (C) 13 + 4 + 1 = 18; (D) 0 + 4 = 4; (E) 12 + 4 + 1 = 17; (F) 1 + 4 = 5; (G) 6 + 4 = 10; (H) 11 + 4 = 15; (I) 2 + 4 = 6; (J) 15 + 4 + 1 = 20; (K) 8 + 4 = 12; (L) 5 + 4 = 9; (M) 9 +4 = 13; (N) 4 + 4 = 8; (O) 3 + 4 = 7; (P) 14 + 4 + 1 = 19.

You can make up squares for very large numbers, for example, the year you were born. With a little practice, and some memorizing, you'll be able to do this mental feat very quickly.

In the **Preparation** section, you were instructed to pencil four sets of numbers at the top of the pad on the inside of the front cover. Each set of numbers is a reminder of the numeric values assigned to the four rows of squares: A, B, C, D; E, F, G, H; I, J, K, L; and M, N, O, P.

Illus. A8 shows the completed magic square in our example. Good luck on mastering this feat of mental agility!

THIS MAGIC SQUARE HAS BEEN ELECTRONICALLY COMPUTED BY THE MAC COMPUTER TO TOTAL 47 WHEN ADDED IN ANY DIRECTION. THE COMBINATIONS ARE:

A, B, C, D   E, F, G, H
I, J, K, L   M, N, O, P
A, F, K, P   M, J, G, D
A, D, M, P   F, G, J, K
I, J, M, N   A, B, E, F
C, D, G, H   K, L, O, P
E, I, H, L   B, C, N, O
A, E, I, M   B, F, J, N
C, G, K, O   D, H, L, P

A 11	B 14	C 18	D 4
E 17	F 5	G 10	H 15
I 6	J 20	K 12	L 9
M 13	N 8	O 7	P 19

Illus. A8

TRICK TELEPATHY

Telepathy, ESP, precognition—little did you know that you possess all of these gifts! You can repeatedly demonstrate them in an entertaining fashion!

Telling Time

The first half of this is a regular trick; the second half is definitely a joke. Ask Carl to look at his watch or a clock (or to visualize a clock) and select two numbers that are opposite one another. He adds these together and tells you the result. You instantly tell him what the two numbers are. You even repeat the stunt a few times.

If you check your watch, you'll see that there are only six combinations:

$$1 + 7 = 8$$
$$2 + 8 = 10$$
$$3 + 9 = 12$$

$$4 + 10 = 14$$
$$5 + 11 = 16$$
$$6 + 12 = 18$$

If you know the total, you know the two numbers. It might take you a moment to solve, unless you thoroughly memorize the possibilities. I devised a simple method to enable you to give out the numbers immediately. At first, it might sound complicated, but a few trials will demonstrate that this method is quite easy. What's more, you'll never forget it.

When Carl tells you his total, divide that by two, and then add three. This gives you one of the numbers. Subtract that number from the total given you, and you'll have the other number. Carl tells you that his total is 14, for instance. Divide it by two, giving you 7. Adding 3 gives you 10, one of the numbers. You announce this immediately. Then you subtract 10 from his total, 14, and you get 4, the other number.

Do this a few times. Now for some silliness. Speed is of the essence in this portion of the stunt. Move right along.

Point to Pete. "I'd like you to note two numbers that are directly opposite each other on a clock face. Got them? Now subtract the lower number from the higher. Okay? Concentrate on that. The resulting number is 6."

Quickly point to Patricia. "I'd like you to visualize two numbers on a clock face that are directly opposite each other. Subtract the lower number from the higher. Concentrate. The resulting number is 6."

Point to another person, and start the routine again. I guarantee you that the group won't let you provide more than three examples of your telepathic ability.

Give 'Em the Slip

Here we have either magic at its finest, or the dumbest trick of all time. Some will think you're a *fabulous* magician.

You'll need eight little pieces of paper, so tear up a napkin or a sheet of paper. Take a pen or a pencil, and, holding one of the pieces of paper in the palm of your hand (so that no one can see it), say, "Will someone please give me a first name?"

You write down the name on the piece of paper, fold the paper, and toss the paper on the table. Take another piece of paper, ask for a name, write on the paper, fold it, and toss the paper on the table. Repeat the procedure for all eight pieces of paper. Mix up the slips and say, "While I turn my head, I'd like you to pick out any one of the pieces."

Someone does so. Then say, "Open it up and look at the name." Again, someone obliges. With head still averted, you say, "The name is Dennis." And, sure enough, you're right.

"Simple case of mental telepathy," you explain. Wait a few moments, gather up the other papers and discard them. If no one objects, you've performed a superb piece of magic.

But if someone troubles to open some of the other papers, he'll discover that the same name is written on each one, because you wrote the first name given on every slip!

In the first instance (if you discard the slips), you've performed a miracle; otherwise, you've presented a comical stunt.

You Can Count on Your Body

This very old trick originally involved several objects on a table and having a spectator think of one of them.

Get Hilda to volunteer, and say to her, "I'd like to point out different parts of my body." As you list each part, you touch it with one hand or the other. "Here we have my right hand, my left hand, my stomach, my throat, my mouth, my knee, my ear. Right hand, left hand, stomach, throat, mouth, knee, ear." Again, touch each part as you name it.

"Now I'd like you to *mentally* spell the part you thought of as I go through the parts again. Start the spelling with the first part I touch, and each time I touch a part, think of the next letter in the spelling. When you've finished spelling the word, say, 'Stop!'"

The first two times, touch any of the listed parts. Then you touch parts in the reverse order of the list: ear, knee, mouth, throat, stomach, left hand, right hand. As you can see, the list progresses from a three-letter spelling to a nine-letter spelling. When Hilda says stop, you'll be touching the exact part she thought of.

Repeat the trick until everyone either catches on or grows tired of it.

Clearly, you may use other parts of the body if you choose, but you must start your list with a three-letter word, and then add one letter at a time to ensuing words.

Another option is to use the parts of someone *else's* body.

The Think-a-Drink Trick

Here is another way of performing the "You Can Count on Your Body" trick.

Effect: Place six white business-sized cards on the table. Printed on the face of each card is the name of a popular drink *(Illus. A9)*. Instruct a member of the audience to mentally select one of the drinks. After he has done so, ask him to silently spell the name of the drink to himself, one letter at a time, as you tap each card in turn. Every time you tap a card, your assistant is to spell one letter. When your assistant reaches the last letter of the drink, he is to cry, "Stop!" To his astonishment, you will be pointing at the card with the name of his drink on it.

Materials Needed:
- Six white business cards. On each card should be printed, in large letters, the name of a popular drink: *tea, milk, water, coffee, limeade, and root beer.*

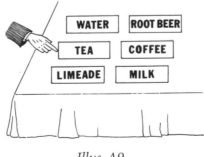

Illus. A9

Presentation: The secret of the trick lies in the fact that the names of the drinks all contain a different number of letters. Tea has three, milk has four, water has five, etc. After your assistant has mentally chosen one of the drinks, instruct him to spell out the name of his drink, one letter at a time, as you touch each card in turn. For the first two letters, you can touch any of the cards. However, starting with the third letter, you must touch the three-letter card, *tea*, for the fourth letter the card *milk*, for the fifth letter the word *water*, etc., until the spectator says, "Stop!"

When you place the cards on the table, mix them up so that the fact that each drink contains a different number of letters is not obvious. Also, use this trick more as a transition from one major trick to another. Do it once and don't repeat it, as the modus operandi will quickly become apparent if repeated too often.

You can also make up a set of these cards using objects other than drinks. You might use colors, rock stars, cars, etc. Tailor the cards to suit your audience.

How Oh-Old Are You?

Give Ethel a pencil and some paper. Turn your back and ask her to write down her age. She may lie, if she wishes.

Let's assume that she writes down 57 as her age. "Please add 70, which happens to be my lucky number. Got it? Now cross out the first digit. For example, if your number is 120, cross out the 1. Now add that digit to your new number. For instance, your number was 120 and you crossed out the 1. So your new number is 20.

Add the 1 to that and you'll get 21."

Ethel has written 57. She adds 70, giving her 127. She crosses out the first digit, 1. This leaves her with 27. She adds the 1 to 27, giving her 28.

You ask for the result, and then say, "Your age is 57. You really didn't have to overstate it that much. Which is it really? 39? 40?" You'll never make anyone unhappy with this approach.

How did you know her age? You added 29 to the result she gave you. She said 28, you added 29, and came up with 57.

If asked to repeat the stunt, you can cause confusion by coming up with different lucky numbers. When 70 is your lucky number, add 29 to get the age. When you use 80, add 19. When you use 90, add 9.

One thing to keep in mind: The total of your lucky number and the person's age *must* be more than 100.

Gotcha!

You'll need a notepad measuring approximately 3" x 5" (7.5 x 13 cm). The sheets should be thick enough so that ink marks won't show through. Let's assume that you're going to predict the result of a hypothetical football game between the "Lions" and the "Bears." On the back of the top sheet, in the exact middle, print the word "Bears."

Now you're ready to make this proposal to the group: "Suppose the Lions and Bears are playing football. I'm going to write down here who I think will win." Holding the pad so that no one else can see, print the word "Lions" in the exact middle of the top sheet. Fold about a third of the sheet upwards *(Illus. A10)*.

Illus. A10

Tear off the sheet, and without letting anyone see the back, fold the top third *under (Illus. A11)*. Toss the folded sheet onto the table. Later, depending on how you open the sheet, you can show either side. Practice the unfolding so that you can readily show whichever side you wish.

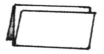

Illus. A11

Ask the group to decide among themselves which team they think will win. When they finally decide, ask, "Are you sure? You can change your mind if you wish." When they're quite sure, unfold the sheet so that they can see that you've correctly pre-dicted their choice. Crumple the sheet and put it into your pocket. Leaving your hand in your pocket, talk briefly about how even you don't understand the nature of your remarkable powers. Casually remove a crumpled paper from your pocket and toss it on the table as you continue to babble.

In nearly all instances, someone will take the crumpled paper and open it up. He'll read, "Gosh, you're nosey!" or some similar message.

That's right. Beforehand you placed a folded and crumpled sheet in your pocket with this message on it. You exchanged the papers in your pocket!

MENTAL MAGIC
WITH MONEY

When you perform a trick where you purport to be using telepathy, you should create the impression that you are actually trying to use your extrasensory powers. Concentrate, hold your hand to your forehead, receive your telepathic message gradually. Good acting heightens the trick's effectiveness and increases the fun.

Heads or Tails #1

Through your mystical powers, you are able to divine whether a spectator has chosen heads or tails. You may repeat this several times.

The lengthy explanation may make the trick seem complicated. Actually, it's quite simple.

You may perform this with any coin denomination, and with any number of coins. Try to use seven to twelve quarters; it's easy to tell a head from a tail, and this is essential.

In this example, assume that you have ten quarters on the table. Count the number of heads showing, noting whether the number is odd or even. You notice that five heads are showing, so you say to yourself, "Odd."

Ask a spectator to assist you. Say:

"While my back is turned, I want you to turn over a coin. When you do, say, 'Turn.' You may do this as often as you wish. And you may do it with the same coin as often as you wish. Just remember to say, 'Turn' every time you turn a coin over. Tell me when you're done."

Turn your back to the spectator, and ask him to begin.

You noted an *odd* number of heads, so when the spectator says, "Turn," say to yourself, "Even." When again he says, "Turn," say to yourself, "Odd." Continue alternating like this until he says that he's done. You need only remember the last thing you said to yourself, "Odd" or "Even." In this instance, say that you are remembering "Odd."

Say, "Please slide a coin away from the rest and hide it under your hand."

When the spectator is ready, turn around. Study the hand under which the coin is hidden, stare into space, glance casually at the coins on the table. All the while, get a count of the number of heads now showing. Again, you note whether the number is odd or even.

You are remembering "Odd." If the number is odd, it is *the same* as the word you have in your mind. If the number is even, it is *different* from the number you have in your mind. Is the coin under the spectator's hand heads up or tails? Easy. Just remember this: *different: head; the same: tail.*

Suppose you just noted that an odd number of heads is showing. You are remembering "Odd." They are the same. Therefore, think of *the same: tail.* The coin under the spectator's hand is tails up. Through extensive concentration, reveal this.

Here's another example. You count the number of coins that are heads up on the table, noting that the number is even. Turn your back. The first time the spectator turns a coin and says, "Turn," you say to yourself, "Odd." Next time, you say, "Even." Next time, "Odd." And so on. When the spectator says that he's done, you remember the last word. In this example, "even." Your assistant hides a coin under his hand. You turn back and count the number of coins that have heads showing. In this instance, the number is odd. You are remembering "Even." They are different. You say, "The coin under the spectator's hand is heads up."

The trick may be repeated several times. You may want to perform the basic trick a few times, and then try this variation. Instead of having your assistant slide one coin in front of him and conceal it under his hand, have him hide *two* coins. Count the heads, as before. If the number gives you a result that is *different*, your assistant has a head and a tail under his hand. If the number gives you a result that is *the same*, the spectator has either two heads or two tails under his hand.

It always goes over well when you tell your assistant that he has a head and a tail under his hand. But it is less effective when you must tell your assistant that both coins under his hand are the same. Instead of doing this, say:

"I just can't get it. Two coins are just too much for me. Please push one out here."

Note what it is when he pushes it out; the other coin is the same. Concentrate, and then tell him what he's still concealing under his hand.

It doesn't matter how many coins you use in this trick. Clearly, the fewer you use, the faster you will be able to determine whether the number of heads is odd or even. Don't use fewer than seven coins, however. Another advantage to using seven coins is that you can talk about the mystical properties of seven, or of how seven has always been your lucky number.

Heads or Tails #2

Here's a simpler version of the preceding trick. Both versions are quite effective, so you may decide to use one or the other. You may prefer to do them both. After doing the first version a few times, say:

"Let's make it more difficult. This time don't tell me when you turn the coins over."

You have a number of coins on the table; the number is irrelevant. You might prefer to use quarters because it's easier to tell heads from tails. Count the number of heads and remember whether the number is odd or even. Suppose that the number of heads is odd. All you need to remember is *odd*.

Say to your assistant:

"I would like you to turn over two coins at a time. Do this as many times as you wish. You may turn over any two, including one or both of the ones you just turned over. Don't let me hear you turn them over, and certainly don't tell me when you're turning them over. When you are done turning the coins over, slide one under your hand. I'm going to put my hands over my ears, so tap me on the back when you're all done.

Turn away and put your hands over your ears. When you turn around after the spectator taps you on the back, count the heads on the coins, noting whether the number is odd or even. Suppose that the number is odd. Since you're remembering *odd*, the two are *the same*. As in the first version, you think:

"The same: *tail*."

Your assistant will reveal a tail when he lifts up his hand.

In this example, suppose that when you turn around, the number of heads on the table is even. This is *different* from odd. You think:

"Different: *head*."

In other words, you use precisely the same code as in the first version of this trick. The only difference is that in this variation, you don't keep track of the number of turns the spectator makes.

Don't neglect to gradually name heads or tails as you get "mental vibrations" from your assistant.

Row, Row

This trick can be performed with coins, poker chips, or other small objects. Let's assume you're working with pennies. There should be at least 20 to 25 pennies on the table.

Get a volunteer and say:

"Let's try an experiment in telepathy. While my back is turned,

I'd like you to make two rows of pennies. The top row should have one more penny than the bottom row."

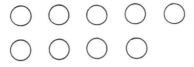

Illus. A12

Show him what you mean by setting up two rows of pennies, five in the top row and four in the bottom row. The rows should look like the drawing in *Illus. A12.*

Push the pennies aside, saying:

"You may use any number you like so long as you have one more in the top row."

Turn your back while he sets up his rows.

Say, "Now name a number that's smaller than the number of pennies you have in the top row."

Suppose he says, "Five."

Say, "Remove that many pennies from the top row."

Pause.

"Don't tell me the number of anything, but do you see the number of pennies left in the top row?"

Of course he does.

"Take that same number from the bottom row."

Then say: "I'm trying to concentrate now, but it's just too difficult. Too many pennies. Would you remove the rest of the pennies from the top row?"

Ask the spectator to concentrate on the number of pennies remaining. Finally, you say:

"I see...remaining in front of you...four pennies!"

You are right.

The trick is automatic. All you do is name one number lower than the number he announced. At the beginning, he said he was taking five pennies from the top row, so at the end of the trick, you came up with "four."

You will want to work it out for yourself, but here's an example:

The spectator lays out two rows; the top row is nine and the bottom row is eight.

```
1   2   3   4   5   6   7   8   9
1   2   3   4   5   6   7   8
```

He takes six pennies from the top row.

```
1   2   3
1   2   3   4   5   6   7   8
```

He notes how many are left in the top row and takes that many from the bottom row.

```
1   2   3
1   2   3   4   5
```

He removes the top row. And you have five left, one less than the number originally removed from the top row.

Naturally, the trick shouldn't be repeated. But you can follow up with the very similar *Give and Take*, immediately following.

Give and Take

You could perform the preceding trick and then do this one. Together they convincingly establish your telepathic powers. This one can, and probably should, be repeated at least once.

You're going to try another experiment in telepathy. Turn your back. This time your assistant is to make two rows of coins, with the *same number* in each row.

Say to your assistant:

"You may add coins or remove coins from either row, using additional coins or discarding coins. You may move coins from one row to the other. But you must tell me exactly what you're doing each time. For instance, if you're putting two more coins into the top row, you must tell me that. If you're transferring three coins from the top row to the bottom row, you must tell me that. And so on."

Here's the secret: As your assistant tells you of his various moves, you follow along mentally, *assuming* that he has seven coins in each row to start with, although you could actually use any number of coins. So at the beginning, say to yourself, "Seven, seven."

Your assistant says, "I removed three from the top row."

Say to yourself, "Four, seven."

There are now four coins in the top row, and seven in the bottom row.

Your assistant says, "I'm transferring two from the top row to the bottom row."

Say to yourself, "Two, nine."

Your helper says:

"I'm adding four to the top row."

Say to yourself, "Six, nine."

Assume that the spectator is done making his moves.

There are more coins on the bottom than on the top, so you say:

"Count the coins on top. Take that number away from the bottom."

This will leave three on the bottom.

"Now please take away the top row."

Concentrate and then announce that the number left is three.

Once more, all you need to do is follow the spectator's moves with your model of two rows of seven coins each.

Suppose that the spectator started with two rows of eleven coins each. He takes three from the top.

```
1  2  3  4  5  6  7  8
1  2  3  4  5  6  7  8  9  10  11
```

He transfers two coins from the top row to the bottom row:

```
1  2  3  4  5  6
1  2  3  4  5  6  7  8  9  10  11  12  13
```

He adds four coins to the top row.

```
1  2  3  4  5  6  7  8  9
1  2  3  4  5  6  7  8  9  10  11  12  13
```

You direct the spectator to count the number of coins in the top row and remove that many from the bottom row.

1   2   3   4   5   6   7   8   9   10
1   2   3

Now he is to remove the top row. The result is three, just as it would have been if he had started with two rows of seven or *any* two rows of coins, so long as they were the same number.

To sum up, follow the spectator's moves, using your model of two rows of seven coins each. When the spectator is done, have him count the shorter row (you will refer to it as the top or bottom row) and remove that number of pennies from the other row. You then have him remove the original shorter row (again, refer to it as the top or bottom row).

If the spectator is making moves so swiftly that you can't keep up, tell him:

"Please slow down. It's very difficult trying to concentrate when you go so fast."

Clockwork

This coin trick is based on an old card trick. In the card trick, the magician seems to declare the number of red and black cards in two piles. In this coin trick, the magician seems to know how many heads and tails are in two groups of coins.

You need twelve coins of the same type. Use quarters because they show up well. You'll also need one odd coin to use as a marker; use a penny because it is strikingly different from the quarters.

Ask a spectator to assist you. Then lay out the quarters in the form of a clock, all of them head side up. Explain, "This is a clock, and this penny marks the quarter that is at 12 o'clock." Place the penny above the quarter (from the spectator's view). *Illus. A13* shows what the spectator sees as he looks at the quarters.

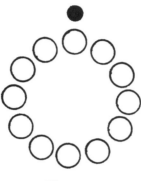

Illus. A13

Turn away, saying:
"Would you please turn over two of the quarters."
Pause, and say:
"Now turn over four other quarters."
Actually, you could simply say:
"Please turn over six of the quarters."
But the other method helps disguise the principle.
Then direct the spectator to turn over the quarters at two o'clock, four o'clock, six o'clock, eight o'clock, ten o'clock, and twelve o'clock. Naturally, give him time to turn over the appropriate coins.

Ask the spectator to slide to one side the quarters at one o'clock, three o'clock, five o'clock, seven o'clock, nine o'clock, and eleven o'clock. Tell the spectator:

"You now have two separate groups of coins. If I have correctly guided your moves, you should have the same number of heads and tails in each group."

Turn around and help the spectator verify that this is so.

You may repeat the trick, varying it somewhat. Again lay out the quarters head side up and mark twelve o'clock with the penny. Turn away. This time have the spectator turn over one coin, then two other coins, and finally three other coins—again, six in all.

Give these directions, leaving time for the spectator to perform the moves:

"Turn over the quarter at one o'clock. Turn over the one at two o'clock. Slide to one side the quarter at three o'clock. Turn over the quarter at four o'clock. Slide away the one at five o'clock. Turn over the quarter at six. Slide away the one at seven. Slide away the one at eight. And slide away the one at nine. Turn over the one at ten. Turn over the one at eleven. And slide away the one at twelve o'clock."

Again, you explain that if you have arranged things properly, both piles should now have the same number of heads and tails.

What you've done is precisely the same thing you did the first time. You have had the spectator turn over six coins and slide away the six other coins.

You need not follow the order given above. As a matter of fact, always make it different. Start at one o'clock and work around the clock to twelve. As you go, use your fingers to keep track of the number you've had the spectator turn over. When you hit finger number six, have him slide the rest aside.

Do you see why this trick works? Don't feel sheepish if you don't; the secret is quite subtle.

Put twelve coins in front of you in a group, face side up. Turn over any six. You have six heads and six tails. Now separate the coins into any two groups of six. Look at group one. Suppose you see two heads and four tails. In group two you will see two tails and four heads—the exact opposite. Obviously, if you turn over all the coins in one group, the two groups will match. This is precisely what happens with this trick.

Slide the two groups together. You have six heads and six tails. Randomly separate the coins into two groups of six. Examine the two groups. It is *inevitable* that you will have the same number of heads in one group as you have tails in other, and vice versa. Turn over all the coins in one group, and the groups will match.

Play with this principle. Maybe you'll find an even better trick.

Your Choice

In this trick you'll correctly predict which of four coins a spectator will choose.

Ask a spectator to assist you. In a row on the table, place a penny, nickel, dime, and quarter. The coins should be about 3" apart. The dime should be the second coin from the spectator's right.

Unknown to your audience, you're holding a dime in a loose fist in your left hand.

Ask the spectator to place his hand on one of the coins. If he is right-handed, chances are strong that he will cover the dime, the second coin from his right. Suppose he covers the dime. Indicate with your right hand that he is to move his hand off the coin. Pick the coin up in your right hand. Hold each hand in front of you in knuckles-up first. Slowly open your hands, showing that you have a dime in each. Smile, saying, "I was right."

If he covers a different coin, say, "And one with the other hand."

Suppose he covers the dime with the other hand. With your right hand, pick up the uncovered coins and set them aside.

Say, "Hand me one, please."

If he hands you the dime, take it in your right hand and complete the trick as before, saying, "I was right."

If he hands you the other coin, take it in your right hand and set it aside with the others. Point to the dime on the table with your right first finger. Then point to your left hand and slowly open it, showing the dime.

Say, "I was right."

Suppose that the spectator covers a different coin with one hand and another different coin with the other hand. Gesture with your right hand that he is to hand you the coins he's covering. When he does, set them aside. Point to the remaining two coins, saying, "Hand me one, please." Proceed as you did in the paragraphs above by pointing.

Run through this trick several times, trying out the various options. It's really quite simple. It's important that you proceed without pause. Most of the time you won't have to bother with the patter: The spectator will cover the dime first.

Cover-Up

You should start with quite a few pennies on the table.

You're going to separate seven pennies, each with a different date, and you will set aside one penny with a date that matches that of one of the seven pennies.

As you check through the pennies for dates, you might say:

"I need several pennies for this experiment. It's very difficult making choices."

Continue in this vein until you have the seven pennies spread out in the middle of the table. Push all the extra pennies aside. Hold up the penny which matches the date of one of the seven.

"This penny is most important. Can I get someone to hold his hand on top of this?"

Set that last penny to one side on the table, date side down, and get a spectator to cover the penny with his hand.

Make sure all seven pennies are date side down.

Get a volunteer to help you. Tell him this:

"We will take turns eliminating the pennies until only one is left. First, I'll cover two pennies with my hands. You choose either hand. We will eliminate the coin under it. Then you cover two pennies, and I'll choose one to eliminate. We'll keep this up until only one penny remains."

You follow this procedure, eliminating all the pennies but one. As each penny is eliminated, you push it to one side. Make sure the eliminated pennies are in a group of their own so that they can be checked later.

At the end, only one penny remains.

Say, "Now let's check the penny I set aside."

Ask the spectator who's holding the penny under his hand to read aloud the date on it. Have your volunteer read the date on the remaining penny. They match, and when the other six pennies are checked, their dates are found to be different.

To accomplish this wonderful result, all you must do is keep track of the penny which matches the one under the spectator's hand. You start the elimination by covering two coins other than the matching one. The spectator covers two coins; if he should cover the matching coin, choose the other hand. Again you cover two coins other than the matching one. And when the spectator covers two coins, you make sure that you don't choose the matching penny. Continue until only one penny is left. Naturally, it is the matching one.

After revealing that the two coins match, you can create a "sucker" ending by feigning reluctance to display the other six pennies. You might gesture towards the coins and say:

"These are unimportant, so we might as well put them with the others."

Probably someone will want to examine them, so you reluctantly give in. If no one says anything, say:

"Oh, well you might as well check the dates."

Some in the audience may be actually disappointed that the dates are all different, but most will be amused.

Money Talks

Although the explanation of this trick may make it seem complicated, actually it isn't. In fact, it's a wonderful teaser which you will be called on to do again and again. The patter is quite important, so some suggestions are offered as the trick is described.

Get a spectator to assist you. Place three pennies and a quarter in a row on the table. Say to your assistant:

"You've undoubtedly heard the expression 'Money talks.' If that's true, a penny would speak in a whisper, and a quarter would be somewhat louder; and I'll try to *hear* that quarter."

Point to the coins.

"I'm going to turn my back. When I tell you to switch the coins, switch the quarter with the penny on either side of it."

Demonstrate a few movements, bringing the quarter to an end position.

"Of course if the quarter is on the end, you must switch it with the penny next to it."

Demonstrate.

"Now arrange the row any way you want, placing the quarter in any position among the three pennies."

When the spectator finishes rearranging the coins, you must casually note the position of the quarter. Suppose the spectator arranges the coins as follows, *from your point of view:*

Illus. A14

To clarify, the quarter is second from his left and third from your left. Here's how you mentally catalogue the row of coins:

R   L   R   L

Illus. A15

"R" stands for Right, and "L" stands for Left. In our example, the quarter is at "R," so all you need to remember is *Right*. The explanation will follow below.

Turn your back, and say, "Switch."

Have the spectator perform *five* switches in a row; then you'll provide further instructions. Pause between switches, and pretend to concentrate. Murmur things like:

"I'm not quite sure. Let's try another switch."

"It's not speaking to me yet. Switch once more."

"Concentrate on the quarter. Maybe one more switch."

"I'm starting to hear it. Switch again."

The idea, of course, is to distract the spectator from the *number* of switches made, which must be exactly five. Keep track of the switches made using your fingers.

After your helper has made five switches, say:

"Obviously, I have no way of knowing where the quarter is. But if you concentrate on it, perhaps it will speak to me."

Both of you concentrate a moment.

Say, "Now remove the coin on *your* right."

This is why you had to remember that the quarter was at the *Right* position.

Pause, and then say, "Make one more switch."

This last switch *always* places the quarter between the two remaining pennies.

Now he must remove the two outside coins. Say, "Take away the coin on the ... right.

Concentrate a moment.

"Take away the coin on the left."

"If money talks," you say, "the coin remaining should be the quarter."

Turn around and look surprised when you see that the quarter is the remaining coin.

"It worked! Amazing."

This trick can be repeated a few times. If you plan to do it three times, vary the procedure the third time. When you come down to three coins, the quarter between two pennies, have the spectator pick up the middle coin. Pause a bit and say:

"Wait a minute! You just picked up *my* coin. The quarter just yelled that it's being smothered."

Turn around, saying, "I believe you're holding the quarter."

Here's why the trick works. Again, here are the possible positions of the quarter (as you look at them):

R   L   R   L

Suppose that the quarter is originally in one of the "R" positions. After five switches, the quarter will be in one of these two positions (as you look at them):

Illus. A16

Tell the spectator to remove the coin at *his* right, and you're left with two possibilities:

Illus. A17

After one more switch, the quarter is in the middle.

Essentially the same thing happens when the quarter starts in an "L" position. The only difference is that, after five switches, you tell the spectator to take away the coin on his left.

Mr. President

When this trick is properly performed, it appears to be real mind reading. To make this really work, however, the magician must convincingly act the role of the mentalist.

Place five coins on the table: a penny, a nickel, a dime, a quarter, and a fifty-cent piece. Say, "Five of our most famous presidents are pictured on these coins."

Touch each as you say, "Lincoln, Jefferson, Roosevelt, Washington, and Kennedy." In your presentation, do *not* use the first names of the presidents; you'll see why later.

Get a volunteer and say to him, "While I turn my back, I would like you to pick up one of these coins. Please hold the coin tightly in your hand, and hold your hand to your forehead as you concentrate on the president you have selected…Lincoln, Jefferson, Roosevelt, Washington, Kennedy."

Turn your back.

You're about to perform a subtle elimination procedure. To do so, you must remember N-O-I-O. These are the letters you will name, in order.

Say, "Are you concentrating on the president? I'm getting the letter 'N.' Is the letter 'N' in the president's name?"

If the spectator says yes, you continue.

If he says no, say, "Yes, it's the letter 'N.' It's in the first name. In fact, it's doubled in the first name. Franklin. You're thinking of Franklin Roosevelt!"

The spectator has said yes, so you say, "The letter 'O'… I'm getting the letter 'O.' Is that right?"

If he says yes, continue.

If he says no, say, "The first name. I see the letter 'O' in the first name. John. It's John Kennedy!"

The spectator has said yes, so you say, "I see an 'I.'" Are you visualizing an 'I'?"

If he says yes, continue.

If he says no, say, "No, no, not the letter 'I.' The eye of the president whose picture is facing to the right. I see the picture of

…President Thomas Jefferson!"

The spectator has said yes, so you concentrate a moment and say, "I'm not getting the name. Please concentrate on the first name only. I'm getting the letter…'O.' Is that right?

If he says yes, say, "The president you're thinking of is…George Washington."

If he says no, say, "Oh, that's my fault! I was visualizing a nickname…Honest Abe. I was getting the 'O' in the word 'Honest.' You're thinking of Abraham Lincoln."

Act this one out with pauses, gradual discoveries, intense concentration—you'll have a little miracle.

When doing the first elimination, be sure to use this exact phrase or its equivalent: "Is the letter 'N' in the president's name?"

If this isn't made clear, a spectator may assume that you are talking about the initial letter of the name.

This may be the only version of this trick that uses all five United States coins.

COIN MAGIC

VANISHES

The magician shows a coin, and it disappears. This is unquestionably the basic coin trick. You should have several ways to accomplish this.

French Drop

One of the oldest of all coin sleights is the *French Drop*. Many people are familiar with it. Done properly, it's an effective, deceptive vanish.

For most of these tricks, the type of coin or coins you use is irrelevant. I recommend, however, that you use a fairly large coin, either a quarter or a half-dollar, when you manipulate a single coin.

Let's try the basic sleight.

With the left hand turned palm up and fingers curled in, hold the coin between the first two fingers and the thumb.

The right hand is palm down as it approaches from above.

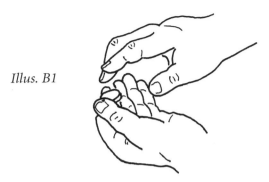

Illus. B1

The right thumb is beneath the coin and the fingers above it, and you close your right hand into a fist as you, presumably, take the coin.

Actually, you simply spread the first finger and thumb of the left hand slightly apart, dropping the coin onto the cupped fingers of the left hand. The right hand, which now supposedly holds the coin, continues to move forward.

Illus. B2

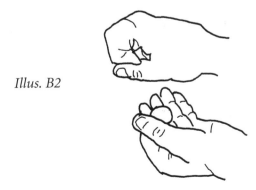

This is one of the simplest coin sleights and probably the best known, but the vast majority of those who attempt it do it badly. Perhaps you've seen someone perform the sleight and present both closed fists, asking you to pick out the one containing the coin.

Sleights should be performed smoothly and naturally. How do you learn to perform a sleight *naturally?* Practice by actually taking the coin in your right fist instead of performing the sleight. Next, perform the *French Drop.* Then, actually take the coin. Continue alternating until, when you perform the sleight, you precisely duplicate the action of taking the coin. I don't recommend practicing in front of a mirror (some performers tend to narrow their eyes so they won't see the sleight, and carry this habit over into performance), bud do check periodically to see if the sleight looks natural. Be sure to try *both* ways in front of the mirror.

You've performed the *French Drop,* and the right fist has moved forward, ostensibly with the coin. What about that left hand? There's a tendency to want to hide the coin, to close the left hand; resist that temptation. Simply drop the cupped left hand naturally to your side. *Don't close the hand;* there's no need to, since the coin is secure there. No one will see it; attention is on the right hand. *But* the coin had better be produced, and soon.

Here's another possibility. Immediately after you ostensibly take the coin with the right hand, point to the right hand with the left forefinger, and then let the hand drop to your side.

French Drop for One

This is a mystifying variation of the *French Drop*, but it's best performed for an audience of one. Ideally, the spectator will be seated and you'll be standing. Otherwise, you'd have to hold the coin rather high, because it must be held close to the spectator's eye level.

The coin (preferably a fifty-cent piece) is held between the thumb and first finger of the palm-up left hand, about a foot from the spectator.

The right hand approaches from above, and the tips of the right second and third fingers push against the right side of the coin, pivoting it around.

Illus. B3

As you complete the revolution of the coin (heads is now where the tails was), several things happen. You loosen your grip on the coin with the left thumb and first finger, and the coin drops onto the cupped fingers of the left hand, and you press your right thumb against the right second and third fingers as though holding the coin.

Raise the right hand in the air, with the back of your hand to the spectator. Snap your fingers, showing that the coin has disappeared. With your left hand, produce the coin with one of the methods given in *Reappearances,* beginning on page 61.

Easy Vanish

There are several ways of pretending to place a coin in one hand while actually retaining it in the other. The following method is one of the easiest to perform, yet it's completely deceptive.

Any size coin will do for this stunt. First, practice the actual placement of the coin, then do the sleight.

Hold both hands out face up, a coin resting on the pads of the second and third fingers of the right hand.

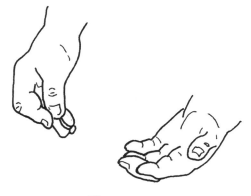

Illus. B4

Move the right thumb so that it holds the coin in place, turn the hand palm down and raise the hand so that it's above and to the right of the left hand *(Illus. B4)*.

Place the coin in the middle of the left palm.

Let go of the coin, and as you withdraw the right hand, fingers still together, close the fingers of the left hand on the coin. As your right hand withdraws, the closing fingers of the left hand should brush lightly against the back of the right fingers.

Illus. B5

When your right hand is a few inches from your left hand, cup the second, third, and fourth fingers, leaving the first finger extended. Tap your left wrist once with your right forefinger, and let your right hand drop naturally to your side. Gradually open the left hand, and, sure enough, the coin is there.

Practice the actual placement several times before you attempt the sleight. Do it very deliberately. You could do a leisurely two-count. Count "one" for placing the coin in the palm, and "two" for tapping the wrist with the forefinger.

For the sleight, you do everything in exactly the same way,

except that at the step where you let go of the coin, simply hang on to it; keep it between the thumb and the second and third fingers of the right hand. Don't forget to tap your wrist with your forefinger, this creates the impression that your right hand is empty. Let your right hand drop to your side.

Now the closed left hand presumably holds the coin, but the coin is actually in the right hand. All that remains is the disclosure of the disappearance, followed instantly by a magical reappearance.

Combined Vanish

For certain tricks, the following vanish is the sleight of choice, for instance, for *Leg Work,* on page 67.

Again, both hands are displayed, palms up. A coin lies on the right fingers approximately one-half inch from the tips. Bring the right hand over and in front of the left hand, with the tips of the right fingers under and touching the back of the tips of the left fingers *(Illus. B6).*

Illus. B6

As the right hand moves up and back, closing the left fingers and presumably dropping the coin, the right thumb grips the coin *(Illus. B7)*.

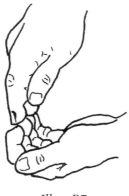

Illus. B7

The right hand continues back a few inches. Cup the second, third, and fourth fingers of the right hand and tap the left wrist with the extended forefinger. In some tricks, this last tapping move may be omitted.

REAPPEARANCES

From the spectators' point of view, one disappearance is pretty much the same as another. In most instances, you apparently place a coin in one hand, but actually you don't. *You* may be enchanted by the notion that each succeeding disappearance is more ingenious and more skillful. Spectators won't be captivated; they'll feel that you've performed the same trick several times.

What's important is the *reappearance* of the coin. Here you can get variety and retain audience interest. I offer suggestions here, and I'm sure that you'll come up with some ideas of your own. You can use most of these reappearances with any vanish.

Slap Through the Leg

Let's assume that you've pretended to place a coin in your left hand in one of the vanishes. Do *not* immediately show the left hand empty. Instead, place your right hand under your right leg and slap the top of that leg with your right hand from behind the leg.

Another version is to slap your left hand against the side of your left leg, then instantly slap your right leg and display the coin at your fingertips, showing that it has penetrated both legs.

If you have performed the *French Drop* (page 53), pretending to take the coin with the *right* hand, simply reverse the hands and proceed as described.

From a Spectator's Ear

Suppose that you've performed the *French Drop* (page 53). You've presumably taken the coin with your right hand, whereas it is actually in your left. Raise your right hand, held in a loose fist, above shoulder level (as though you were holding the coin up), letting your left hand drop naturally to your side. Then snap the fingers of the right hand. Turn the palm towards the audience, showing that your right hand is empty.

Produce the coin from a spectator's ear. Simply reach toward the spectator's ear with your cupped left hand, the back of your hand toward the spectators. When you are about an inch or so from the spectator's ear, slide the coin to your fingertips with your thumb, and almost touch the ear with the coin. Instantly, push the coin into sight as you pull the hand away from the ear.

Another way to show that the coin has vanished is to drop the right hand to belt level and make an upward tossing movement, as though throwing the coin into the air. You can then produce the coin from the spectator's ear.

Pass Through the Head

This reappearance may be used with any vanish. Suppose that you've pretended to place a coin in your left hand, whereas it is actually in your right hand.

Approach a spectator. Reach out with your left hand, back of the hand toward the audience, pretending to hold the coin between your thumb and fingertips. Lightly push your fingers against the side of his or her head, above the ear.

Meanwhile, you have let the coin drop onto the fingers of the right hand. Reach out with your right hand, its back to the spectators, so that they can't see that you hold the coin between fingers and thumb. Immediately after you have pushed against the side of the spectator's head with your left hand, produce the coin at your fingertips from the corresponding spot at the other side of the subject's head, using your right hand.

Cough It Up

This reappearance provides a little drama and a touch of humor. Before performing the sleight, bend over so that people can see the top of your head. Touch the middle of your head, saying:

"I don't know if you can see it from there, but I have a little hole in the top of my head. Yes, people are right about me, but it does come in handy now and then."

Perform your choice of vanish, then bring the empty hand, lightly closed as if you are holding the coin, above your head. Open your fingers as you slap the top of your head. *Immediately* bring the hand holding the coin to your mouth as if to cover a cough, and let your left hand drop to waist level. Cough, and let the coin fall from the hand at your mouth, catching it in the hand at your waist. This trick usually gets a laugh, and always delights children.

You may wish to indicate the hole in the top of your head after performing the vanish. As you explain about the hole, simply touch the middle of your pate with the forefinger of the hand that holds the coin, holding the coin loosely cupped against your palm with the rest of your fingers. While less direct, this can serve to apparently demonstrate that the hand is empty, and you can then proceed to complete the trick as above.

Catch as Catch Can

This excellent method of retrieving a vanished coin is deceptively easy to perform. The timing must be precise, however. Spend as much time practicing this as you would a difficult sleight.

Using any vanish, pretend to place a coin in the left hand. The coin must be held in the palm of the right hand. The left hand is closed; the right hand holds a coin in the palm. Raise both hands to head level, backs of the hands to the spectators. The fingers of the right hand should be spread. Don't worry about the coin; it will stay in the right palm, unseen and quite secure.

Make an upward throwing motion with the left hand, spreading the fingers. Follow the flight of the invisible coin with your eyes, asking, "Where'd it go?"

Make a quarter turn to the left as you do three things: turn the left hand palm towards the audience at waist level, fingers open; drop the right hand to waist level, letting the coin fall onto the left fingers; with the left hand, reach out to the left and grab the invisible coin, saying, "Here!"

Quickly bring the left fist down towards the right hand and, when the left fist is about a foot away from the right hand, make a throwing motion, as though tossing the coin into the right hand. Instantly move the right hand slightly upward, bouncing the coin an inch or so into the air, simulating the catching of the coin, followed by a little bounce. Display the coin at the fingertips, both hands held up, palms toward the audience.

The little bounce when you catch the coin in the right hand is critical. The audience sees the coin hop into view as though it had just arrived. Practice the timing.

Behind the Knee

Very few reappearances can match this one. A coin disappears. You attempt to pull it from your leg using your empty left hand; no luck. You try from the right side of your leg with your empty right hand; still no luck. You try with the left hand again, and there's the coin!

You may use any vanish to (ostensibly) place a coin in your left hand, while retaining the coin in your right hand. The right hand drops casually to your side, as the left hand is shown to be empty.

Immediately drop the left hand, palm outward, to slightly behind the left knee, where you grip a little fabric of your trousers between your fingers and thumb. Apparently, you are trying to pull the coin from the fabric. Let the fabric slide through your fingers, showing that your hand is empty. Return the hand to slightly behind the knee.

You have let the coin drop so that it's resting on the fingers of your right hand. With the back of your right hand to the audience, bring your right hand to the rear of the right side of the knee. Again, you are going to grip the fabric of your trousers. Before you do this, pass the coin to the fingers of the left hand. Simply drop the coin off the ends of your right fingers as you grip the fabric. The coin falls onto the tips of the left fingers, which hold it against the back of the knee.

Pull out the fabric with the right hand, trying to extract the coin. Let the hand slide off, showing that it's empty.

Try again with the left hand. As you pull out the fabric, the coin is held behind it. Gradually, pull the coin out *(Illus. B8)*.

Apparently, you have shown both hands empty, but you've then produced the coin.

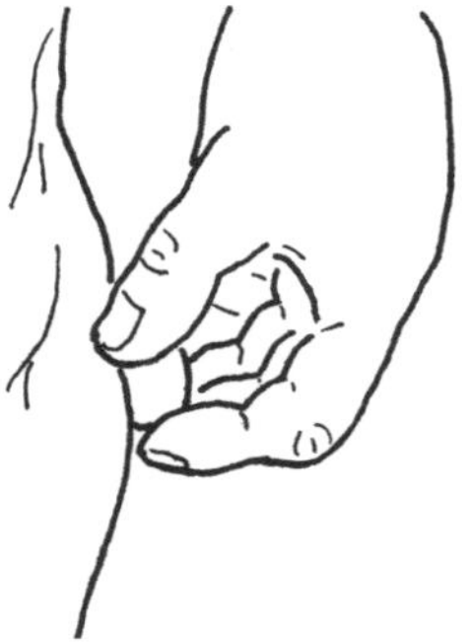

Illus. B8

Leg Work

For this trick, the *Combined Vanish* works best. See page 59.

Place your left foot on a chair. Or, if you have an excellent sense of balance, you could raise your knee in the air. Another possibility is to be seated in a chair.

Place a coin—preferably a penny—on your raised left leg near the knee, and another several inches nearer your torso.

Place the back of your open left hand on top of the nearer coin (the one closer to your torso).

Pick up the other coin and pretend to place it in your left hand, using the *Combined Vanish* (or one of the other vanishes). As you move your right hand away, let the coin fall onto your cupped fingers, so that you will be able to pick up the other coin between your first finger and thumb.

Raise your closed left hand to your mouth, and blow into your left fist. *At precisely the same time,* pick up the other coin with the first finger and thumb of your right hand.

Hold both hands in front of you in two fists, separated by a foot or so. As you perform this trick, you might want to say:

"Like people, coins are sometimes attracted to each other. Here we have two coins, complete strangers, as far as I know."

Revolve both hands slowly several times, and then open them, showing that both coins are in your right hand.

"But look. Apparently, there was real magnetism between them."

This trick shouldn't be done speedily. Strive for smoothness and naturalness. The moves should flow. When the moves become automatic, you can perform several repetitions without fear of discovery.

Why does this trick work? Blowing into the left fist while picking up the coin with the right hand tends to confuse spectators. They simply can't follow what you're doing.

Seven Cents

You need seven pennies for this trick. This trick can be repeated several times; no particular skill is required.

Show that your hands are empty. Give seven pennies to a spectator. Have him verify that there are only seven.

Take the pennies back and hold them in your cupped left hand. Say to the spectator:

"I'd like you to hold out your left hand so that we can check the count. When I've placed the seventh penny in your hand, I want you to close your hand immediately so that no pennies can escape. Ready?"

Pick up a penny with your right hand, holding it between your second finger and thumb. Your hand should be *palm down* as you place the penny into the palm of the spectator's hand, counting, "One." Place another penny into his hand the same way, making sure that you clink it against the penny already there. As you do so, count, "Two." Continue in the same way with pennies three, four, and five.

Place the sixth penny into his hand in the same way, counting, "Six." Make sure to clink it against one of the coins, *but withdraw your hand, retaining the coin.* Since the back of your hand is to the spectators, no one will see that you still have the coin. Besides, your next move captures everyone's attention.

Immediately, with your left hand, toss the remaining coin into his hand, counting, "Seven." He should close his hand instantly. If he fails to do so, help him with the left hand by placing it beneath his fingers and pushing upward, saying, "Close your hand!"

Quickly show that your left hand is empty and tap his fingers with your left fingers. Bring your right hand under his left and push the coin against it. Bring your hand away, displaying the penny at your fingertips. It's as though you had pulled it through the back of his hand!

Tell the spectator:

"There seems to be a hole in your hand. Let's try it again."

Take the pennies and repeat the trick at least once. Repeating it three times is just about right.

Aspiring magicians have a tendency to feel that the move involved in this trick is much too bold, and that they won't get away with it. At the time you keep the penny, all attention is on the delivery of the seventh coin and the closing of the hand.

The key is to keep a consistent rhythm as you count the coins into the spectator's hand. The sixth coin should be counted out in precisely the same way as the first five.

This is a very difficult trick to practice, since it's difficult to duplicate the actual action by placing coins on a table, for instance. You'll probably have to rehearse with a trusted friend. Don't be surprised if you fool your friend on your first try!

Throwback

Display a coin in your right hand. Point to it with your left hand.

Swing both arms down so that they go slightly behind your back, and then instantly swing them up again, your right hand tossing the coin into the air about two feet or so. Both hands are back to the audience. Your left hand has its first finger extended so that it can point to the coin which has been tossed into the air.

Your right hand catches the coin, and both arms swing down again, going behind your back. Again the coin is tossed into the air and caught by your right hand as your left first finger points.

When your hands swing behind your back the third time, the coin is tossed from your right hand to your left. Both hands come up as before, and the invisible coin is tossed into the air, with your left first finger pointing.

In great puzzlement, look at your empty right hand as you show its palm to the audience. At the same time, let your left hand drop to your side, fingers loosely curled around the coin. *Immediately* say, "Ah, there it is!" With your right hand, reach to a spectator's left ear as though to produce the coin. Close your fingers and thumb as though grasping the coin. Then, looking puzzled, show the hand empty. "Wait a minute," you say, as you reach out with your left hand and produce the coin from his right ear.

There are other possible conclusions. You could do *Behind the Knee* (page 65).

The Magic Circle

A coin is placed in a handkerchief, which is held in the left hand. The coin mysteriously disappears. This is an excellent old trick that would be enormously improved if you could show that the coin is not in your right hand, but you can't.

This method gets rid of the coin, enhancing the trick and also providing additional entertainment. For the trick to work, all spectators must be directly in front of you.

Hold your left hand palm up and drape a handkerchief over it. The hand should be at the center of the handkerchief. One corner of the handkerchief should rest on your wrist.

Place a fifty-cent piece in the center of the handkerchief so that you can grip the coin through the fabric with your left hand, fingers at the front and thumb at the back. About two-thirds of the coin should be showing (*Illus. B9*).

With your right hand, grasp the corner of the handkerchief which is resting on your wrist and bring it forward over the coin. As the handkerchief covers the coin, turn your left hand over so that your fingers point to the floor. Move your right hand away and point to the coin under the handkerchief, and say:

"Did everyone see the coin?"

Reverse the motions just described, so that the fifty-cent piece is again on display. Move your left hand from side to side so that all may see the coin.

"A fifty-cent piece," you declare.

Again cover the coin as you did before the last step. But, as your right hand reaches its lowest position, release your grip on the coin, dropping it into your cupped right fingers *(Illus. B10)*.

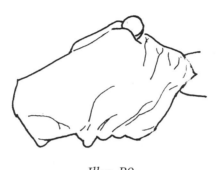

Illus. B9

Illus. B10

As before, point to the presumed coin under the handkerchief, raising the handkerchief to arm's length above your head. The coin, of course, is held by the cupped second, third, and fourth fingers of your right hand. Casually let your right hand drop to your side.

As you raise the handkerchief above your head, start turning around clockwise. With little shuffles of the feet, turn in a complete circle, staying in the same place. Your left hand continues to hold the handkerchief high above your head. Throughout the turn, you will talk, saying something like this:

"Have you ever heard of the magic circle? Well, before your very eyes I am making a magic circle right now. There is no extra charge for this feat. I'm happy to do it for you. Who knows? Maybe someday you'll learn to make a magic circle of your own."

By this time, you should be facing the front again. While making your "magic circle," you did something extremely sneaky. When your left side was towards the audience, you dropped the coin into your right trouser pocket. Or, if that pocket wasn't available, you might have tucked it under the top of your trousers or your skirt.

You're still holding the handkerchief (and supposedly, the coin) at arm's length above your head. Reach up with your right hand and take a corner of the handkerchief between your first and second fingers. Let go with the left hand and let the handkerchief fall, held only at the corner by the right fingers. This is a very showy climax.

You're holding one corner of the handkerchief between two fingers of your right hand. Switch the grip, so that you're holding it between your thumb and first finger. Take an adjacent corner between the thumb and first finger of your left hand and spread the handkerchief between the hands, palms to the audience. Reverse the position of your hands, showing the other side of the handkerchief. Give the handkerchief to your audience for them to examine and show both sides of both hands.

Say, "Thank goodness the magic circle worked!"

While you make your magic circle, all attention is on the handkerchief you are holding aloft. This misdirection of the audience's attention is perfect for ditching the coin.

SLEIGHTS & STUNTS

"The hand is quicker than the eye." Old-time carnival performers would bark out this line as part of their patter, and it became perhaps the best-known line in magic. Unfortunately, this has led many aspiring magicians to believe that incredible speed and skill were essential to performing sleight-of-hand tricks. With the vast majority of sleights, this is absolutely untrue. As you will see, you don't have to be fast, but you *must* be smooth and natural.

Using Your Head

Choose a person to assist you and proceed to cause a coin to vanish. Everyone knows how you did it, *except* your assistant. This generates considerable amusement. But then, in a humorous climax, you also let your assistant in on the secret.

Select as your assistant a good sport. Have him stand facing you, both of you with your sides to the audience.

Display a quarter or a fifty-cent piece. Say to your assistant:

"We're going to perform a little experiment to test your reflexes. On the count of three, I will place the coin in your hand,

and you should close your hand and grab the coin. But you'll have to be fast. So hold out your hand palm up, please. Ready?"

Hold the coin between your thumb and fingers. The coin should be near the tips of the fingers, but it shouldn't extend beyond them. You're now going to rapidly swing your arm up so that your hand is about 2" above your head. Immediately swing your arm down again and lightly touch the coin to the palm of the spectator's hand. As you near the hand, say, "One!"

Repeat the motions, saying, "Two!" Repeat the motions, saying, "Three!" Your assistant should grab the coin. But whether he does or not, leave the coin in his palm and quickly withdraw your hand. Casually show that your hand is empty and ask your assistant, "Did you get it?" Of course he did. Compliment him on his reflexes. Take the coin back, saying, "Let's try it again."

Repeat the actions through a count of one and two. As your hand comes above your head the third time, place the coin right on top of your head. Instantly bring your arm down as before, saying, "Three!"

As before, quickly withdraw your hand. Ask, "Did you get it?" Of course he didn't, although he may think he did. Have him open his hand. Display both of your empty hands. Say, "Magic." The audience should be amused, and your assistant should be quite puzzled.

Pause for a bit, basking in the glory of your achievement. Then say, "Thank you, thank you," and take a little bow, letting the coin fall off your head to the floor. Snap your fingers in mock disgust.

"Doggone it! I always forget."

When you swing the coin above your head and down to your assistant's hand, always keep the back of your hand toward your assistant.

Rarely, an assistant (particularly a tall one) will know what you've done. Since you're performing more of a stunt than a magic trick, this discovery doesn't diminish the fun. If this happens to you, feign great chagrin and confess that your helper is too smart for you. Then pretend to take the coin in one hand, performing one of the vanishes. Extend the hand presumably containing the coin to your assistant, saying, "Here, you keep the money." Invariably the spectator reaches to take the coin, and you show the hand empty. "Those are the breaks," you say, and then you cause the coin to reappear from somewhere.

Heads Up

Use a fifty-cent piece or a quarter for this stunt. A tricky movement is required, but you should master it after five or ten minutes of practice.

The idea is to convince spectators that you have a double-headed coin.

Hold the coin, the heads side up, in the palm of your right hand, slightly to the left of the middle of your palm.

Say, "Have you ever seen a two-headed coin?"

Display the coin so that all can see it. Hold both hands palms up, your left hand about 6" from your right hand and about 2" lower than your right hand.

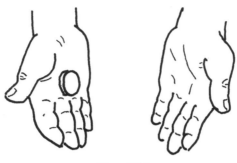

Illus. B11

Jerk your right hand quickly to the left, letting the coin slide off your right palm and onto your left palm. Obviously, it falls face up *(Illus. B12)*. In the same motion, slap your right hand palm down on your left palm.

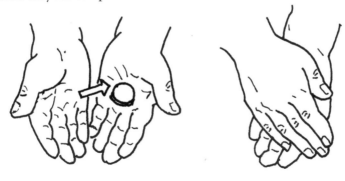

Illus. B12   *Illus. B13*

This move is done quite rapidly. The illusion is that you've turned the coin over onto your left palm. Lift up your right hand to show that, evidently, the other side of the coin is also a head.

Using the same move, return the coin to your right hand. Show the coin.

Return the coin to your left hand, and then back to your right. You've adequately demonstrated that you have a two-headed coin. You should have a strong ending. Say:

"Many people have offered me a dollar for this fabulous two-headed coin."

Address one of the spectators:

"Would you be willing to pay a dollar for this?"

As you say this, place the coin in your left hand so that the tail side is up. Since you don't want anyone to see the tail side, use the legitimate version of the *Easy Vanish* move (page 57). Hold the coin between thumb and fingers in your right hand, and the coin will naturally turn over as you place it in the palm of your left hand. Close your left fingers over the coin as you withdraw your right hand.

If the spectator says that he would be willing to pay a dollar, open your left hand, saying, "Bad choice." Display the coin on your left palm, showing the tail side. Then lift the coin up and show both sides.

If the spectator says that he wouldn't be willing to pay a dollar say, "Good thinking," and display the coin as above.

Easy Call

To perform this stunt, you must learn a tricky move. The move isn't difficult, however, and the effort will be well rewarded.

Use a half-dollar, although a quarter will do. Flip the coin about 18" into the air with your right thumb, catch the coin, and then slap the coin onto your left wrist. *Illus. B14* shows how to hold the coin when you're about to flip it.

Illus. B14

As you flip the coin and slap it onto your wrist a few times, say:

"Wouldn't it be wonderful if you could always tell the way the coin would end up?"

You then call heads or tails, as you flip the coin. Catch the coin, slap it onto your wrist, and, sure enough, you're right.

Actually, you do not *flip* the coin, although it certainly looks like it. You look at the coin lying in your hand. Suppose that the head side is up. You'll catch it the same way. When you slap the coin onto your wrist, the coin will be turned over. So, as you perform the pseudo-flipping action, you call tails.

Here's the trick move. Hold the coin in your hand as before, but with a slight variation. Your thumb is held back from the coin, and your first finger is above the tip of the coin.

Illus. B15

Don't *flip* the coin into the air, but propel it upwards in a quick hand movement resembling the regular flipping motion. As you propel the coin upwards, let the side of the coin tick against your first finger. This will give the coin a wobbling motion which looks very much like a regular spin. Naturally, the coin never actually turns over; it returns to your hand with the same side up as when you tossed it.

This move is easy enough to practice, and it shouldn't take you long to get the knack.

Stuck with A Penny

Get a good sport to assist you. Take a penny at the edges and hold it up to your forehead, tail side toward your forehead. Rub it into your forehead, turning the coin in place in a slight circular fashion. The coin will adhere to your forehead. Now say:

"It's easy enough to take the penny away when you use your hands, but otherwise it can be very difficult."

Wrinkle your face up, trying to dislodge the penny. Assume

that you aren't successful. Take the penny from your forehead and say to your assistant:

"I wonder if *you* could do it. Okay?"

Again holding the coin at the edges, rub it into your assistant's forehead, *but take the coin away,* dropping your hand to your side. Say:

"Without using your hands, give it a try."

The audience should derive considerable amusement from your assistant's facial contortions as he tries to dislodge the coin.

After he tries for a while, casually begin flipping the penny and catching it. Eventually, he should get the idea and hold his hand to his forehead.

"Good heavens," you might say. "You made it disappear."

Occasionally, your assistant will notice immediately that you did not leave the penny on his forehead. You might say:

"You're right. To tell you the truth, I just didn't trust you with it."

It was once believed that the penny had to be moistened or it wouldn't adhere to the forehead, but this is not true.

Flip-Flop

You may perform this trick using either five half-dollars or five quarters. Half-dollars are better because they're easier for spectators to see. Not many people carry half-dollars, however, so if you're going to borrow the coins, use quarters.

Place the five coins on your left so that they overlap. Heads and tails should alternate. Say,

"Heads and tails intermixed. Let's see what we can do about that."

Meticulously push the coins into a stack with your right fingers and thumb. Hold the coins at the ends of your fingers and thumb as you lift the coins a few inches above your left hand.

Illus. B16

You're now going to drop the coins one at a time onto your left palm. Assume for a moment that the coins are heads up, tails up, heads up, tails up, heads up. When you drop the first one, you will release pressure from both fingers and thumb simultaneously; the coin will fall directly into your left hand, still heads up. With the second coin, however, you will release only the thumb. This will cause the coin to pivot off the fingers and turn over, also landing heads up. The third coin is dropped regularly, the fourth caused to turn over, and the last dropped regularly.

Show that all the coins are now heads up. The stunt may be repeated.

It isn't easy learning how to drop the coins properly. First, you'll have to determine the correct distance separating your left and right hands. Second, you must figure out how you lessen the thumb pressure so that the coin will pivot off your right fingers and turn over; you must develop a certain "touch." The solution is practice!

Quick Transpo

This trick is fast and effective. A coin held under one hand magically moves under the other hand. Two versions of this trick appear in the book. *Quick Transpo* is somewhat easier, and it's done standing up. The other, *Hand to Hand*, follows.

Flip a coin (any size) into the air a few times to keep spectators from focusing on the key move. Hold both hands out and palms up, displaying the coin in the right hand about 1/2" from the ends of the fingers.

Simultaneously slap your two hands against your stomach, tossing the coin from the right hand so that it lands under the left. Because of the simultaneous movement of the hands, the coin arrives just before the left hand smacks against your stomach.

Illus. B17

Rub your right hand against your stomach vigorously, as though rubbing the coin away. Remove your right hand from your stomach and show that it is empty. Turn over your left hand, letting the coin drop into it. Display the coin.

Don't hesitate to try this trick. There's a good chance that you will succeed in a good throw on your first attempt. You'll get the knack in less than five minutes.

Hand to Hand

This is a slightly more difficult version of *Quick Transpo*. You'll show a coin in each hand, yet when you slap the coins down on the table, both will end up in the same hand.

Both hands are placed palms up on the table, a coin resting on each hand. The coin in your right hand lies on the right side of the hand, above the thumb and below your first finger, while the coin in your left hand is resting on the second joints of the fingers. The positioning is important, as you're about to toss the coin from the right hand to the left hand, and you don't want a telltale clink. Also, placing the coin on the right side of the right hand makes it easier to throw the coin.

The two hands should be separated by a few inches more than the width of two hands, or about a foot.

With a quick movement, turn both hands over and inward, smacking them palms down on the table. As you do so, toss the coin from the right hand so that the coin lands under the descending left hand.

The technique of the throw is a bit tricky. As the proper method is described, please remember that the entire move takes only a fraction of a second. Raise both hands about 2" above the table before turning them inward and slapping them down. The coin is tossed as the palms face each other. The coin is slapped down, along with the other coin, with the left hand. Meanwhile, the right hand also smacks the table, right next to the left hand. Keep in mind that you must *throw* the coin from the right hand.

To end the trick, make a circular motion on the table with your right hand; then turn your right hand over and move it aside, showing that the coin has vanished. Lift your left hand, revealing both coins.

When done properly, the passage of the coin is absolutely invisible. About ten minutes of practice should do it.

The position of the coin in each hand has been emphasized. The trick can also be performed with both coins on the palms and both coins on the fingers. Experiment to find which method works best for you. The trick can be performed with any coin up to the size of a quarter.

Once you develop the proper timing, you can perform the trick with any small object—dice, poker chips, etc.

Coins and Cards

Every experienced coin magician performs a version of this trick. Coins mysteriously pass up through a table, appearing under a playing card or under a piece of cardboard.

Most versions call for considerable skill and sly moves, requiring countless hours of practice. This variation is very easy, yet completely deceptive.

Required are four pennies that look alike and two playing cards—preferably poker-size, because these cards are wider than "normal" cards. You can perform this trick on a bare table or on a table with a covering on which a coin will slide easily. The critical move involves sneakily sliding a coin, so a nubby tablecloth will make a proper presentation impossible. If need be, set a large magazine or a file folder on the table.

Lay out four pennies in a square. The pennies should be about six inches apart. Hold the two cards face down, one in each hand.

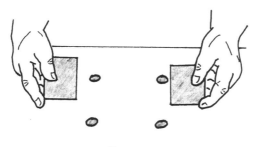

Illus. B18

Set the card in your *right* hand on top of the upper-left penny, retaining your grip on the card. You explain:

"For this experiment to work, we must get the precisely correct magical combination. We can cover a coin with one card, or we can cover it with two."

Set the card in the left hand on top of the other card, retaining your grip on the card.

Illus. B19

Slide the card in your right hand to the right, covering the upper-right coin, still retaining your grip on the card.

"Cover two pennies separately…"

Set the card in your left hand on top of the other card, again keeping your grip.

"…or cover one with two cards."

Slide the card in your right hand down to cover the lower-right coin, keeping your grip, and say:

"Cover two pennies separately…"

As before, set the left-hand card on top, retaining your grip, and say:

"…or cover one with two cards."

Slide the card in your *left* hand to the left, covering the lower-left coin. The back of your middle fingers of your left hand, at the knuckle below the fingernails, should be resting on the penny.

"Cover two pennies separately…"

Set the card in your right hand on top, keeping your grip on it.

"…or cover one with two cards."

Now for the key move. Slide your left hand up to cover the upper-left penny with the card. Along with it, slide the penny which is resting under your fingers.

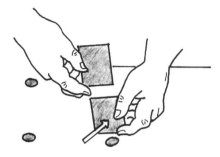

A coin is being slid forward under the card.

Illus. B20

Let go of the card. Two pennies are now resting under it. As soon as the upward movement of the card in your left hand leaves enough room, drop the card in your right hand, presumably covering the lower-left coin.

As you perform the upward movement of the left hand, say:

"Cover two pennies separately…"

You have now dropped both cards.

"That's it!" you declare. "The right combination."

All of the above is down quite rapidly, without pause.

Casually draw back your left hand and let that hand fall into your lap. At the same time, pick up the upper-right coin in your right hand. Hold it up, and announce:

"Let's try this one first."

Bring the coin under the table and tap the underside of the table with your second finger. Try to tap with the end of the fingernail to provide a somewhat metallic sound. Later you'll be tapping *without* a coin, so this sound must be repeated each time.

As you bring your right hand back, toss the penny into your left hand, where it lies on the fingers. Without pausing, bring the right hand out. Reach toward the upper-left card with your palm up. The idea is to show that your hand is empty (without being too obvious). Lift the card off the two pennies.

"Good! It worked."

As you say this, bring the card back to your left hand, which takes it slightly below table level. Under the card, of course, you're holding a penny with your left fingers.

Immediately move your right hand to the two coins, and pick them up and hold them in the air. As you place the card and coin (that are in your left hand) down in the upper-left position, rattle the coins in your right hand, and say:

"Two pennies."

Your left hand now withdraws to the relaxed position on your lap. Your right hand drops the two coins onto the back of the card you just placed down.

The rattling of the coins in your right hand misdirects the spectators' attention from your placement of the card with the coin underneath.

With your right hand, pick up the penny in the lower-right corner, and say:

"Now we'll try this one."

Take the coin under the table, tap, toss it into your left hand, and bring out your empty right hand. Move your right hand palm up to the card in the upper-left corner. Tilt the card so that the pennies on top slide off. Now move the card away, showing that another penny has passed through the table. As before, your right hand moves back and places the card in the left hand, which holds a penny underneath.

Promptly move your right hand forward, pick up the three pennies on the table, and hold them in the air. As you place the card and penny down in the upper-left position, rattle the coins, and say:

"Three pennies."

Drop the pennies on top of the card you just placed down.

The position of the objects on the table should be as follows: In the upper-left corner, you have a card with one penny under it and three pennies on top of it. In the lower-left corner is a card with no coin under it.

Here is the swindle. Place the cupped left hand a few inches below the table, directly behind the card in the lower-left corner. With fingers on top and thumb at the back, slide the card slightly off the table. As soon as the edge of the card clears the table, lift the end of the card about 1" with your thumb. Perform a sweeping motion toward yourself, apparently sweeping the penny off the table into your cupped left hand. Close the left hand as though you were now holding the coin.

"And now this one," you say.

Simultaneously perform two actions. Bring your left hand under the table and tap the underside of the table with your second finger, and then turn the card in your right hand face up and toss it to the right of the other card. This will obscure your sneakiness.

Bring your left hand out and reach palm up toward the card in the upper-left corner. Tilt the card, sliding the three pennies off. Lift the card, showing that the last penny has penetrated the table. Turn the card face up and toss it on top of the other face-up card. Show both sides of your hands, and gather up your materials.

Since this is a fast trick, spectators are likely to be quite dazzled. You may well get a request to repeat it. Simply shake your head and say:

"No, I could never get exactly the right combination again."

To learn this trick, go through it slowly, omitting nothing. Every move has its purpose. Leave out one move and the trick may fail.

You'll know that you're ready to perform the trick publicly when you can go through it quickly and without pause. Performed rapidly, this trick has enormous impact as one coin after another passes through the table and under the card.

Practice your patter as you practice the movements.

This trick is an excellent example of the "one-ahead" principle, which is used in quite a few tricks. Such tricks work because the "dirty work" is done before the spectators are ready to look for it.

Classic Coins Through the Table

Here's a version of one of the most famous coin tricks of all. The effect is truly astonishing. Under the most impossible conditions, the performer seems to pass three coins through a solid table.

The key move requires precise timing; this will take considerable practice. But it will be worth it, for this trick can establish your reputation!

Place six quarters and one half-dollar on the table. Place the quarters in two parallel vertical rows of three each. The rows should be several inches apart. At the top of the row on the right, place the fifty-cent piece. From your viewpoint, the coins should be lined up to look like the drawing below.

Illus. B21

"We are using seven coins," you explain, "because seven is my lucky number. Sometimes."

You simultaneously pick up the two rows, the one on the left with your left hand, the one on the right with your right hand. Start at the top of each row and work toward you. With the right hand, pick up the fifty-cent piece first, and place it on top of the upper quarter. Both are placed on top of the second quarter. And all are placed on top of the near quarter. At the conclusion, the coins are held between your thumb and your fingers, your thumb against the fifty-cent piece. Raise the coins so that they're on edge, resting on the table.

Meanwhile, the left hand has picked up the row on the left, starting with the upper quarter. No attempt is made to pile the coins. At the end, they're held in a loose fist. Turn your hand over so that the back of your hand rests on the table.

Slide your right hand forward to the middle of the table. Tap the fifty-cent piece against the wood, and say:

"The table is very solid on top."

Move your right hand under the table. Set the pile of coins on your leg. Take the fifty-cent piece off the pile, reach under to the middle of the table, and tap the underside of the table with the coin. Say:

"And—surprise, surprise—it's also solid under here."

To cover the slight pause when you leave the quarters on your leg, you might laboriously move your body closer to the table, as though you were trying to reach further under the table; then do the tapping.

Immediately after tapping beneath the table, bring your right hand back to the table, holding your hand in a loose fist. Place your hand so that the back of the hand rests on the table. The hands should be separated by a hand's width plus a few inches.

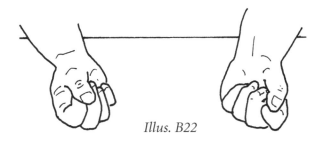

Illus. B22

Roll your left hand clockwise, opening it and slapping its coins to the table. Immediately roll your hand back. Your hand is still open so that all can see that it is empty. Say:

"Three coins in this hand."

Turn your left hand over and gather up the three quarters with your fingers. The hand is back up. The coins are resting on the table, loosely held between the tips of your fingers and the heel of your palm.

Here's the trick move. Two things take place simultaneously: Your left hand lets go of its coins and then rolls counterclockwise as it slaps the fifty-cent piece on top of the three quarters. Immediately roll your right hand back, still open, and say:

"And four coins in this hand."

Pick up the coins with your right hand, holding the coins in a loose fist. As you do so, say:

"A total of seven…perhaps my lucky number."

Bring your right hand under the table. Pick up the coins off your leg, adding them to the ones already in your right hand. As before, move your body closer to the table to cover the brief pause. Bring your right hand with its coins to the middle of the underside of the table.

Slide your left hand to the middle of the table. Turn your hand over and slap it palm down on the table. At the same time, shake your right hand so that the coins jingle. Turn over your left hand, showing that it's empty, and that there are no coins on the table. Bring your right hand from under the table, in a loose fist. Turn your hand over and spread the seven coins out on the table. Say:

"It worked! Seven is my lucky number."

One reason that this trick works so well is that fifty-cent piece in your right hand. After you've slapped the fifty-cent piece on top of the three quarters on the table, spectators make an assumption that you were holding a fifty-cent piece and three quarters in your right hand, and since there are three quarters and a fifty-cent piece on the table, these must be the same coins you held in your right hand.

The basic move must be practiced until you fool even yourself. To get the timing just right—rolling the left hand out of the way just as your right hand is slapping down the fifty-cent piece— practice first *without* coins. When you do add the coins, the move will be much easier to perform.

Remember that you're *not* performing a trick move. Do not tense up. Some performers get anxious just before performing a move, and this nervousness serves as a virtual announcement that something tricky is coming. The idea is that you are just *showing* the coins held by each hand; try to treat it as casually as that.

Don't repeat this trick for the same audience. Consider the requests to repeat the trick as a form of applause. Take a bow and proceed to another trick.

In your patter, don't mention that you are going to try to pass coins through the table; there's no need to put the spectators on guard.

The real key to proper performance of this trick is confidence. If you practice until the moves are automatic, you will have that confidence.

INTRIGUING NON-SLEIGHT TRICKS

A rich variety of effects is available when performing with a deck of cards. Unfortunately, there are a limited number of coin effects. Granted, any number of methods may be used to accomplish an effect, but an audience does not necessarily appreciate your versatility. A coin trick generally takes less time to perform than a card trick. After performing coin tricks for ten minutes or so, you'll probably have done every possible effect. Unless, of course, you have thrown in a few extraordinary tricks requiring no sleight-of-hand tricks such as these following. Do not confine your routines only to sleight-of-hand effects. In a Shakespearean play, comedy heightens tragedy and vice versa. In coin magic, sleight-of-hand effects can be mixed with "non-sleight" tricks, enhancing both.

To Coin a Phrase

The following trick was originally a card trick. Say, "I have developed the ability to estimate perfectly the number of coins a person takes. I do this in a single glance."

Engage the service of a friendly spectator. Tell him:

"Grab some pennies, and I'll demonstrate."

The spectator grabs several pennies.

"Hide them," you say. "And I'll take some."

You grab a handful of pennies.

"Now I'll turn my back. You count your pennies, and I'll count mine."

You both do so. When you turn back, you say:

"I have the same number of pennies you have, three left over, and enough more to make your pennies total twelve."

Repeat the statement.

Let's suppose that the spectator took eight pennies.

Say, "Let's count them together."

He counts his in front of him, as you count yours separately. The coins need not be counted one on top of the other.

As the two of you count, you say aloud:

"One, two, three, four, five, six, seven, eight."

When finished, you say:

"I said, 'Three left over.'"

Count off three pennies to one side.

"And I said, 'Enough left over to make your pennies total twelve.' You have eight there."

Count from your hand onto his pile.

"Nine, ten, eleven, twelve."

You are out of pennies. You are exactly right. You had the same number he had, three left over, and enough more to make his pennies total twelve.

Basically, you have baffled the spectators with a semantic trick.

All you did was to make sure that you had several more pennies than the spectator did.

When you counted your pennies, you discovered that you had fifteen. You mentally subtracted three (for the number left over), and came up with the number twelve. You then told the spectator that you had the same number, three left over, and enough more to make his pennies total twelve. In effect, you told him that you counted your pennies and that you had fifteen; you merely stated it in a subtle way.

Note that at the end you count the pennies onto the spectator's stack. This is the touch that makes the trick work. Somehow, it keeps the victim from realizing that you are *actually* saying:

"I have twelve pennies and three left over."

Once more, all you have to do is to make sure that you have a larger number of pennies than the spectator has. Next, count the pennies, subtract a suitable small number (two, three, or four) for misdirection, and then make your statement.

Let's try one more example. Suppose the spectator grabs a dozen or so pennies. When you count your pennies, you discover you have nineteen. You might say:

"I have the same number of pennies as you have, two left over, and enough more to make your pennies total seventeen."

We'll say the spectator has ten coins. Count aloud as you each count your pennies into separate piles. Set two aside—"two left over."

Then say, "You have ten there."

Count the rest of yours onto his pile, starting with eleven. And, of course, you run out of pennies when you count out the seventeenth.

The Farmer's Will

This is more of a puzzle than it is a trick, but the climax is quite surprising, and the story still entertains.

You say, "An old farmer had two things he valued: his mules and his sons. He had seventeen mules and three sons. These pennies will stand for the mules." Count seventeen pennies onto the table. Ask a spectator to check the count.

Say, "When the farmer died, he left his seventeen mules to his sons. He left one-half to his oldest son, one-third to his second oldest son, and one-ninth to his youngest son. Now the sons didn't know much about math…or anything else, for that matter. But they were smart enough to consult a lawyer. The lawyer had a high school education, so he knew that he couldn't divide up seventeen mules that way. So the lawyer cheerfully donated one mule of his own."

Add another penny to the group on the table.

"At the price he was charging the sons, he could afford it."

Gesture toward the coins on the table.

"So now there were eighteen mules. He gave one-half to the oldest son. That's nine mules."

Count out nine pennies and push them into a separate pile.

"He gave one-third to the second oldest son. That's six mules."

Count out six pennies and push them into a separate pile.

"And he gave one-ninth to the youngest son. That's two mules."

Count out two pennies and push them into a separate pile.

One penny remains in the middle of the table. Point to it, saying, "And the lawyer was amazed to find that he got his mule back."

The trick is based on the fact that the farmer did not actually leave all his mules to his sons; he left only 17/18 of them. He left 1/2, 1/3, and 1/9; in other words, 9/18, 6/18, and 2/18. 9, 6, and 2 add up to 17; thus, 17/18.

Too Many Pennies

In its original version, this was a game at which the spectator seldom (if ever) won. In this version of the trick, the spectator *never* wins, and the presentation provides considerable amusement.

Suppose that you have a fairly large number of pennies on the table. Count out 13 and push the rest aside.

"We'll use 13 pennies," you say.

"As you know, some people consider 13 an unlucky number. So I need a volunteer who's not superstitious."

Josh with the group until you get a volunteer.

Address your helper:

"I challenge you to a game of Skunk. We have 13 pennies here. You can take one coin or two coins. Then I take one or two coins. We keep on until only one is left. Whoever has to take the last one is a Skunk. You start this time. I'll start next time. And let's go as fast as we can. Ready, set, go!"

The spectator is skunked no matter what. Let us say the spectator takes two pennies; you take one. If he takes one, you take two. You continue doing this until there is one coin left on the table, and it's the volunteer's turn.

"Too bad," you say. "You were skunked."

Clearly, the spectator can perform the same feat, if you're the first one to choose and *if* you play with the same number of coins. So let's change the number of coins.

Gather the 13 pennies into a group.

"Too many pennies for you," you say.

"How many do you want to throw out—one or two?"

Set aside one or two pennies, depending on his choice.

"Now it's my turn to start first," you say.

If he chose to set aside one penny, take two. If he chose two, take one. This means that he will be choosing from 10 pennies, and he can't win. You continue to take two when he takes one, and one when he takes two. Again he ends up with the last coin.

"Skunked again," you declare sorrowfully, gathering the coins again.

"You know why? Too many pennies!" you say.

Casually, set aside one or two pennies, whichever will reduce the total number to ten.

"That should be better. Go ahead. Take one or two."

It doesn't matter what the volunteer does. When you follow the same procedure as before, he can't win when he begins choosing from seven pennies.

"Skunked again," you say, collecting the seven pennies.

"You know why? Too many pennies. How many should we throw out—one or two?"

Set aside the number he indicates. It's your turn first. If he chose to set aside two, take one; if he chose one, take two. He has to choose from four and he can't win.

"Skunked again. You know why?"

He may answer, "Too many pennies."

Regardless, you say, "No, no, the problem is—*not enough pennies!*" Push all the pennies back into the center and say:

"We'll change the rules. You get the first turn, and you can take as many pennies as you want."

It shouldn't take him long to figure out that his best bet is taking all the pennies but one.

"I'm skunked!" you declare. "Doggone it, I was hoping you wouldn't think of that."

A Western Tale

Most people enjoy a trick with a story to go along with it. This trick, requiring no sleight of hand, is a good change of pace from snappy coin disappearances and reappearances.

You need seven pennies and one quarter. No penny should look markedly different from the others. Lay out five of the pennies on a table (or the floor, for that matter) like this:

Illus. B23

Set the quarter off to the right side, and set the two remaining pennies near it.

"I'd like to tell you a little Western story," you say, "using these coins for markers. The five pennies I've laid out here are prize cattle, gathered in a corral. The quarter over there is big Lenny, the rancher who owns the cattle. He's in the ranch house."

Indicate the two pennies you set aside, saying:

"And these are two range tramps."

Point to one of the pennies.

"One evening this range tramp arrived at the ranch and asked Lenny to put him up for the night. Lenny said, 'All right. You can stay in one of the barns. But don't get any funny ideas about rustling my cattle, or I'll blow your head off.' So the tramp went into the barn."

Open your right hand.

"This is the barn."

Pick up the penny and hold it in your closed right hand.

"Coincidentally, another range tramp rode in and asked the rancher if he could stay the night. Lenny said, 'Well, I already got a tramp sleeping in my good barn. You can stay in the other one. But don't get any funny ideas about rustling my cattle, or I'll blow you to pieces.' So this tramp went into the other barn."

Open your left hand.

"This is the other barn."

Pick up the penny and hold it in your closed left hand.

"But, of course, the tramps decided to steal the cattle and go off with them early in the morning. So they took them one by one."

Deliberately take a penny in your *right hand*. Then take one with your left hand. Continue alternating until all the pennies are in your hands. As you take the pennies, each hand should be in a fist, with the palm down.

Reach over with your right hand and move the quarter a bit closer to where the pennies had been originally laid out.

"Lenny may have looked dumb, but he was suspicious of those tramps, so he decided to go outside and have a look. Of course, the tramps heard him stomping around inside the ranch house, so they quickly returned the cattle to the corral."

Return the pennies to their original positions, first one from your *left hand,* then one from the right, and continue alternating until all are returned. You now have two pennies in your right hand.

Raise both fists as you say:

"And, of course, the two sneaky tramps remained in the barns."

This is quite important, for it creates the impression that a coin is in each hand.

Edge the quarter near the pennies with your right hand.

"Lenny saw that the cattle were all right, so he returned to the ranch house."

Move the quarter back to its original position.

"Naturally, the greedy tramps stole the cattle again."

As before, alternate hands as you take the pennies, starting with your *right hand.*

"But Lenny was still suspicious. He grabbed his rifle and tip-toed out to the corral."

Move the quarter to where the pennies had been laid out.

"Lenny was pretty quick on the uptake. He noticed right away that the cattle were missing. So he decided to check out the barns.

Only one way could those tramps save their lives: if they were together in one barn, and the cattle were together in the other. And sure enough, in *this* barn…"

Open your left hand.

"…were the two tramps. And in the other barn…"

Open your right hand.

"…were the five cattle."

Shake your head.

"I'll be darned if I know how those tramps did it."

The trick is automatic; just follow the directions. Remember to take pennies with your *right hand* first both times. When you put them back, start with your *left hand*.

This is a perfect choice after you have performed a number of sleight-of-hand tricks. Spectators tend to deceive themselves by watching for sleight of hand. Lenny, of course, is merely window dressing. Obviously, the trick should be done only once; a repetition risks discovery.

Squeeze Play

For this, you must prepare a special coin, and you must learn a fairly simple sleight. The effort is well worth it, for you'll have a funny trick you can perform on any occasion.

Place a coin in someone's hand. That person squeezes the coin so hard that it bends.

Prepare the coin by placing it halfway in a vise. With a large pliers, bend the coin somewhat. Always carry the coin in your right-hand pocket, and you can perform any time. In that same pocket, you should have a handkerchief.

Start by putting your hands in your pockets. Grip the bent coin in your curled right third and fourth fingers. Remove your hands from your pockets as you ask someone to lend you a coin of the same value as your prepared coin. Take the proffered coin with your right hand, gripping it between your thumb and your first and second fingers. Don't be afraid that anyone can see the bent coin.

Toss the borrowed coin into your left hand. Pick out a spectator who's known for his frugality. Clyde, for instance, is quite thrifty. Ask him to hold out his hand. "Now when I put the coin in your hand, hold it really tight." With your left hand, place the coin in his hand. Take the coin with your right hand, gripping it between your thumb and your first two fingers, as before. Now you'll perform a sleight known as The Bobo Switch. Presumably you once more toss the coin into your left hand; actually, you retain the borrowed coin and toss the bent coin into your left hand, where you hold it in a loose fist *(Illus. B24)*.

Illus. B24

Your right hand, of course, holds the borrowed coin. Immediately make a tight fist with your right hand and shake your fist up and down, as though with the intensity of your squeezing. "You have to really squeeze it. Let's try again."

With your left hand, place the bent coin into his hand. By guiding with your left fingers, make sure he closes his fingers on it immediately. Meanwhile, you've let your right hand drop to your side, fingers loosely cupping the borrowed coin.

Reach into your right-hand pocket. Leave the coin there as you remove the handkerchief. Shake the handkerchief open, as you say, "Squeeze really hard, because I'm going to try to make the coin disappear." Cover his hand with the handkerchief. Make mystic waves over it. "Hocus-pocus! The coin's now gone." Whip the handkerchief away. "Please open your hand."

He does so, "Good heavens, look at that! You squeezed it so hard you bent it out of shape. Sorry, I can only make *normal* coins vanish."

Let everyone get a good look at the bent coin and then put it away.

Rolling a Coin

Few things are as impressive to spectators as the ability to roll a coin over the back of your fingers. It is, in fact, fairly difficult, requiring considerable practice. But you can learn it if you have determination and a little patience. And once you master the stunt, you'll be able to use it forever.

It's best to practice over a bed or a couch, or sitting at a table. It gets terribly tiresome picking the coin up off the floor. The best coin to use is a half-dollar, although a quarter will do.

Most of those who attempt the stunt try to roll the coin well down on the fingers. Actually, the coin is rolled just below the knuckles, where your fingers begin.

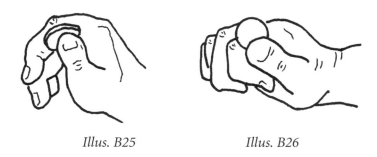

Illus. B25   *Illus. B26*

The coin is balanced on your right thumb *(Illus. B25)*. Note that your hand is slightly cupped. The coin is brought next to your first finger, where the coin is lightly pinched between your thumb and first finger *(Illus. B26)*.

Your thumb pushes the coin up until it drops on the back of your first finger *(Illus. B27)*. Note that your other fingers are raised, preparatory to doing their job.

Your second finger is lowered, clipping the end of the coin and tilting the coin upwards *(Illus. B28)*. As your first finger is raised, the coin falls on the back of your second finger. Your third and fourth fingers are raised.

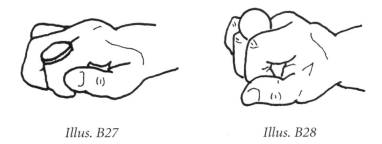

Illus. B27   *Illus. B28*

Your third finger clips the edge of the coin, and then lowers, turning the coin over *(Illus. B29)*.

Now comes the hard part. The coin rests on the back of your third finger. Lift your fourth finger quite high, grasping the coin. Slide your third finger up as you lower your fourth finger, letting the coin slide partly through *(Illus. B30)*.

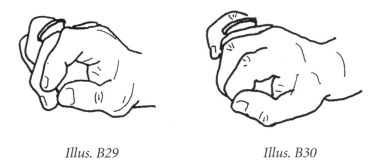

Illus. B29   *Illus. B30*

Bring your thumb under your hand and let the half-dollar rest on your thumb *(Illus. B31)*.

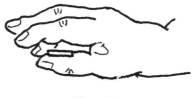

Illus. B31

The thumb brings the coin back, and you're ready to roll the coin again. For best effect, do it several times.

Once you know the moves, strive for a smooth, rolling effect. It works best when you don't watch your hand. This is particularly true when you haven't done this trick for a while. Just let your reflexes take over.

FLASHING FINGERS MAGIC

HAND JIVE

In this chapter all the supplies you need are at your fingertips.

Disjointed Digit

This trick works particularly well for children, but most adults are also amused by it. Apparently you remove the first finger of your right hand.

"I have some amazing feats for you. Actually, they're not feats, but hands. Just watch these magical fingers."

Wiggle your fingers, demonstrating their amazing flexibility. Position your left hand so that your fingers point down and the back of your hand is toward the spectators. Tuck your left thumb into your left palm. Bring your left hand in front of your right. Bend in the first finger of your right hand. Your left hand, of course, conceals this. Rest your left hand on the back of your right hand, fingers still down.

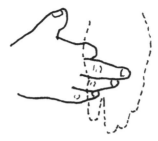

The broken outline shows the position of your left hand.

Illus. C1

Say, "Watch carefully."

Twist your left hand upward, raising the second, third, and fourth fingers. The first finger stays down, hiding the fact that your left thumb is bent inward. The illusion is that your left thumb is the outer joint of your right first finger.

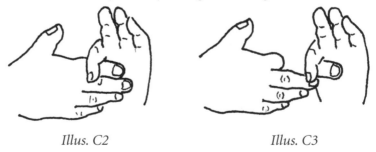

Illus. C2   *Illus. C3*

Move your thumb along the surface of your right second finger several times, demonstrating that the outer joint of your right first finger is separated from the rest of your finger. Then, extend your left fingers again and straighten out your right first finger, grasping it in your left hand. Twist your right hand several times in a semicircle, "repairing" your finger. Hold up your right first finger and waggle it, showing that it's fully restored.

Incredible Shrinking Finger

You can not only remove one of your fingers, you can also shrink one.

Hold up your left hand straight, back of your hand to the onlookers. Grip the little finger of your left hand with your right hand. The first finger and thumb of your right hand hold the top knuckle. The remaining fingers of your right hand are cupped outward.

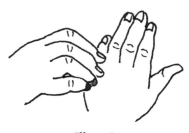

Illus. C4

Push downward with your right thumb and first finger, holding the top of your finger straight. At the same time, however, bend the lower knuckle of your little finger outward. You're concealing this bend with your second, third, and fourth right fingers.

Very slowly, push your little finger down, laboriously reducing its size. The illusion is quite realistic, since the tip of your finger remains pointing upward, and the finger slides down next to straight, extended fingers.

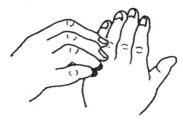

Illus. C5

Agonize as you pull your finger back up. Repeat the reduction. You might even try it a third time. Finally, pull your finger back up, grasp it with your right hand, and rub the finger vigorously. Then show your left hand, moving all the fingers to show that everything is as it should be.

Go Away

Some readers may remember this stunt from their childhood. It's amusing to those who've seen it before, and amazing to those who haven't.

You should be seated at a table. Tear off two bits of paper from a napkin, a tissue, or a paper towel. Moisten the bits of paper and stick one on the fingernail of each of your first fingers.

Place the tips of your first fingers on the edge of the table. Bouncing the two fingers rhythmically, you chant line one: "Two little birds sitting on a hill…"

Bounce the right finger as you say, "One named Jack, …"

Bounce the left finger as you say, "One named Jill."

"Go away, Jack." As you say this, swing your right hand up and past your head. During the swing up, fold in your first finger and extend your second finger. Instantly bring the hand down to the table, displaying the second finger.

Immediately say, "Go away, Jill." Perform the same switching action with your left hand. No one has time to observe what you actually did, because you proceed without hesitation to the next step.

Swing up your right hand again, and switch fingers again as you say, "Come back, Jack." Instantly do the same with your left hand, saying, "Come back, Jill."

Do not repeat the stunt.

The key is to perform the stunt *rapidly*. Once you start, the whole sequence should last no more than ten seconds. A few minutes' practice should give you complete mastery.

Here's the rhyme in one piece:

Two little birds, sitting on a hill,
One named Jack, one named Jill.
Go away, Jack. Go away, Jill.
Come back, Jack. Come back, Jill.

Let's Go to the Hop!

Since the principle here is the same as that of *Go Away* (see previous trick), avoid doing both tricks for the same group at the same time.

Use any one of the following: a colored rubber band wound around your finger several times; an address label, moistened and attached to your finger; a scrap of thin paper (napkin, tissue), moistened and stuck on your finger; or a plastic bandage.

Use the second finger of your right hand. Let's assume you've wound a colored plastic bandage around your second finger. Extend the first two fingers of your right hand. Make sure that the other fingers are well folded in, and that your thumb is out of sight *(Illus. C6)*.

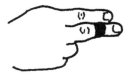

Illus. C6

Hold out your left hand palm up; your right hand should be about 8" (20 cm) above. Bring down your right hand to your left hand, displaying briefly the extended two fingers of your right hand. Leave your fingers there for only a fraction of a second—just long enough for onlookers to see them; then bring up your right hand to its original position. As you bring your right hand down again to display your fingers, fold in your first finger and extend your third finger *(Illus. C7)*.

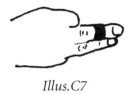

Illus. C7

"Watch it hop!" you say. Bring up your right hand again, and, as you bring it down, switch fingers once more. Repeat the switch several times *rapidly*. The illusion is that the label (or bandage) is hopping back and forth between your fingers.

Revolving Wrist

This brief, extraordinary stunt is a real reputation-maker. Apparently, you're either magical or double-jointed, for you can turn your hand completely around in a manner that's physically impossible.

To start, you must be wearing a suit jacket or sport coat, or the equivalent. For example, a sweater with long, loose sleeves will do.

Kneel down, press your hand against the floor, and turn your hand 360 degrees. It's quite impossible, and it looks ridiculous. When people see you do it, they'll either laugh or gasp.

The secret is quite simple, however, and you'll accomplish the feat easily on your first try. "Ladies and gentlemen," you might say, "I've been practicing magic for some time. As a result, I've gained astonishing control over various parts of my body. Let me show you." Kneel down. Grasp your right sleeve with your left hand so that you can hold the sleeve in place while performing your maneuver. Turn your right hand palm-up and twist that hand counterclockwise as far as you can. Rest the *back of your right hand* on the floor *(Illus. C8)*.

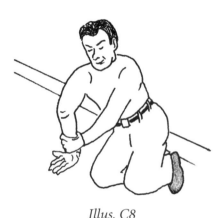

Illus. C8

You should be feeling some strain in your arm and wrist, but that sensation will be quite brief, for you'll begin the maneuver immediately. Very slowly rotate your arm clockwise, holding the sleeve so that it stays steady. Your hand, still pressed against the floor, also turns clockwise, of course. You strain a bit at the end to bring your hand to precisely the position it was in at the beginning. *Illus. C9* shows your hand at various phases of the move.

Illus. C9

Leave your hand in its final position for a few seconds, and then stand up, shaking your hand and arm.

Your audience asks, "How did you do that?" Don't tell them. If you do, you'll turn an astonishing feat into an insignificant little trick. *Don't repeat this trick*—at least not during that performance. Retrospectively, spectators assume that you started with your hand palm-down; don't destroy that illusion! The secret isn't well known, so keep it that way.

Sticky Knife #1

This *old* stunt is a perfect introduction to *Sticky Knife #2* (see next trick). Ancient it might be, but this golden oldie will still provide oodles of fun.

Hold a table knife on your left palm with your left thumb *(Illus. C10)*. Grip your left wrist with your right hand. Turn over your left hand, revolving your left hand in your right hand, which remains still. As you do this, turn your hand downward, so that your left fingers point toward the floor. At the same time, extend your right first finger so that it holds the knife. Now stick out your left thumb, so that all can see it *(Illus. C11)*.

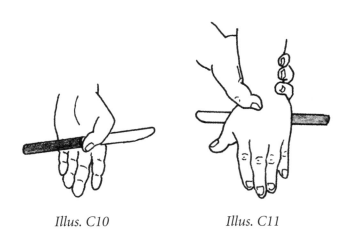

Illus. C10   *Illus. C11*

Move your hands together, back and forth. The knife mysteriously clings to the palm of your left hand. Stop the movement and then precisely reverse the movements you performed when turning over your left hand. First, bring your left thumb onto the knife. Then revolve your left hand, palm up, as you return your right first finger to the side of your wrist.

Repeat the trick, if you wish. You might even consider teaching it to interested spectators. The next knife suspension, however, you won't teach; it's much too good a trick.

Sticky Knife #2

Hold up a table knife and say, "I'll now glue this to the palm of my hand." You attach the knife to your hands by interlocking your fingers, so that the second finger of your left hand is actually slid into the palm of your right hand, while your remaining fingers interlock alternately. As you interlock your fingers, slide the knife under your left second finger so that it's held secure against your right palm *(Illus. C12)*. Don't perform this procedure in plain sight. If you're sitting at a table, take the knife under the table and attach it to your hands. If you're standing up, simply turn away for a moment while you perform the "dirty work."

Illus. C12

Bring your hands and the knife into sight, the back of your hands toward the spectators, and the knife perpendicular to the floor. Hold your thumbs down so that onlookers will get the impression that your thumbs are holding the knife. Move your hands from side to side. "See? The knife is glued on." If no one comments about your thumbs, say, "You seem skeptical. The thumbs? Not at all." Raise your right thumb above your hand. "See? One thumb." Lower your right thumb and raise your left thumb. "And there's the other thumb."

Move your hands from side to side with your left thumb raised. If no one raises an objection, pretend to hear one. "Both thumbs? Oh, all right!"

Raise the other thumb. What? Your thumbs aren't holding the knife? But how…?

Wave your hands about, moving them backward and forward, side to side. Even tilt your hands, bringing them almost level, making sure no one can see your sneaky second finger, the one that's gripping the knife.

Abruptly separate your hands, taking the knife in one. Set down the knife and show both sides of your hands. No stickum, no rubber bands—just sheer magic!

This stunt may also be performed with a pencil, but I find it to be hard on my second finger.

The Levitating Knife

Effect: This is one of those delightfully entertaining impromptu effects that you can nonchalantly present between courses at your next dinner party. Interlock the fingers on both your hands and place them, palms down, on top of a dinner knife. When you raise your hands in front of you, the knife appears to be clinging to them.

At this point, both of your thumbs are hidden behind your fingers and everyone assumes that they are holding the knife against your palms. Tell them that this is not so, and raise your right thumb. They will say that your left thumb is now holding the knife. Move your right thumb back down behind your fingers and raise your left thumb. They will, of course, say that your right thumb is now holding the knife.

Repeat this back and forth several times, and then finally in exasperation raise both your thumbs to show them how wrong they are *(Illus. C13)*. Shake your hands vigorously. The knife will still cling to them. Suddenly, pull your hands apart and let the knife fall to the table. Turn your hands palms up so that your dinner guests can see that they do not conceal anything that could have caused the knife to cling to them. How did you do it?

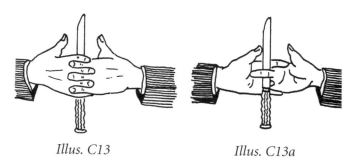

Illus. C13   *Illus. C13a*

Presentation: The secret lies in the way you interlocked your fingers. Although no one is about to count your fingers, in reality only nine of them are showing *(Illus. C13)*. When you interlock them, do it in such a way that the second finger of the right hand is curled into your palm *(Illus. C13a)*. When you pick up the knife, make sure that it goes under this finger, where it will be held in place until you unlock your fingers at the end of the trick.

This is a surprising trick, and one that you should have a lot of fun presenting.

Dippy Die

To perform this trick, you'll have to memorize a bit and practice a little, but no particular skill is required, and the entertainment value is enormous.

A little preparation is required. Prepare a 3" x 5" (7.5 x 13 cm) file card in advance, or use a business card.

In either case, you must take a pen—a marking pen is best—and make little circles on the card, so that the card somewhat resembles a domino. Be sure to color in the circles so that they can be easily seen. On one side, draw two circles, as shown in *Illus. C14.*

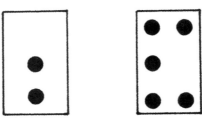

Illus. C14   *Illus. C15*

Turn over the card, as though you were turning the page of a book. On this other side, draw five circles, as shown in *Illus. C15*.

Let's assume that you're sitting around with friends. If you're going to use a business card, casually mark the card while chatting, letting the card rest on your tilted left hand (assuming you're right-handed), shielding what you're doing. In a restaurant, as you mark the card, you can rest it on your raised menu. Incidentally, the printing on one side of the business card shouldn't be a problem; just make sure that you mark the printed side with the two dots.

The key to this stunt is the way you hold and turn the card. For clarity, the illustrations will show the use of a file card.

"Did you ever play card craps?" you ask, keeping your card out of sight. Your friends are likely to answer no.

"Me neither. Until the other night. I met a stranger in a restaurant, and he asked me that very question. 'Did you ever play card craps?' I said, 'No.' He said, 'Nothing to it. I have a magic card that's just like a die. It's a perfectly flat card. On one side is a 1, on the other is a 2, on the other is a 3, on the other is a 4, on the other is a 5, and on the other is a 6.' I said, 'That's impossible.' He said, 'No, that's magic. Here's the way the game goes: We look at both sides of the card. If the two sides total 7, you lose the bet. Then I do it again, doubling the bet. And if I get a 7 this time, you lose...*providing* I get a 7 with two numbers different from the first ones. If I don't, I lose.' I said, 'You've got a bet,' and I put down some money."

Take out the card and hold it in your left hand, so that the number, from the spectator's view, seems to be 6. *(See Illus. C16).*

Illus. C16

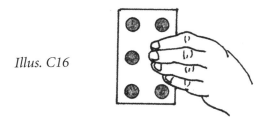

All the remaining illustrations for this trick will be from the spectators' point of view.

Say, "6 on one side." Bring up your right hand, fingers behind covering the bottom dot and thumb in front *(Illus. C17)*. Quickly rotate your right hand counterclockwise, letting go with your left hand. You're now apparently displaying a 1. Say, "And 1 on this side. 6 and 1 are seven. I gave the man the money."

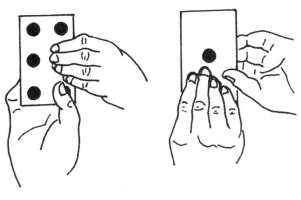

Illus. C17   *Illus. C18*

"I said, 'Now we'll double the bet. Let's see you get a 7 with two numbers different from the first ones.' And he did it."

Grip the card with your left hand, thumb on the front and fingers on the back *(Illus. C18)*. Your fingers should cover the spot on the left side. Rapidly rotate your left hand so that the back of your hand is toward the spectators, and the card is turned end for end. As you do so, let go with your right hand. The spectators are now looking at 4 dots *(Illus. C19)*. Say, "4 on one side."

Illus. C19

As before, grip the bottom of the card with your right fingers on the back of the card and right thumb in front. Turn the card so that the back of your fingers are to the front. You're apparently displaying 3 dots. Say, "And 3 on this side. 4 and 3 are seven. I gave the man the money."

Without changing your grip, drop your hand to your side as you say, "I told the fellow, 'That's fine, but how about giving me a turn with the card?' He said, 'Okay, I'll give you two tries. Each time double or nothing. So I grabbed that card and went to work."

When you display the numbers for your turn, the handling will be different. Grasp the card in the usual manner with your left hand, (as shown in *Illus. C18*, page 130). Turn the card end-for-end, displaying an apparent 6 spots. Say, "6 on this side."

Now for the different handling. Turn your left hand so that the card's long side is parallel to the floor. With your right hand, grip the card on the right side, fingers on the back of the card and right thumb in front *(Illus. C20)*. Turn over the card with your right hand. Immediately turn your right hand palm up so that you display the spots as shown in *Illus. C21*.

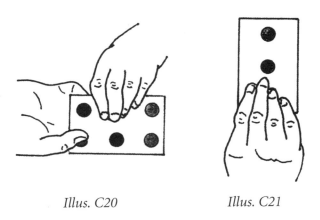

Illus. C20   Illus. C21

Say, "And 3 on this side. 6 and 3 are nine. I lost again, but I bet one more time."

Revolve your right hand, turning it palm down. Take the left-hand grip in the usual manner (*Illus. C22*). Turn the card end-for-end, displaying 4 spots. Say, "4 spots on this side."

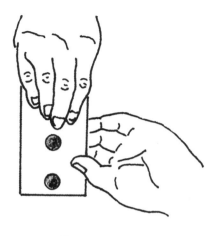

Illus. C22

As before, turn your left hand so that the card's long side is nearly parallel to the floor. Your right hand grips the card on the right side, fingers on the back of the card covering the dot and your right thumb in front. Turn over the card so that you display 1 dot. Say, "Whoops! One dot on this side. 4 and 1 are five. I lost again."

At this point, if you wish, you can tear the card into little pieces, saying, "I was so disgusted I tore up the card and called it quits." Some spectators may be baffled as to how you accomplished this magical feat. With children, I almost always close by tearing up the card.

Here's the way I prefer to finish:

Drop your hand to your side, saying, "The stranger said, 'Let's have another game. It's my turn with the magic card.' I said, 'Sure.

Double or nothing. Only this time, no tricky turns. Just drop the card on the table…and then turn it over on the table.' He said, 'Okay,' and took the card."

Drop the card on the table. "5 dots on this side." Flip the card over. "And 2 dots on this side. 5 and 2 are seven."

Rip the card to shreds. "The moral is, 'Never gamble with strangers.'"

Notes: If you use a business card rather than a file card, you can adequately hide the dots with one or two fingers, rather than three.

The moves aren't really difficult. Mark a card and follow the directions. In short order, the moves will be second nature to you.

PAPER MAGIC

The Beelzebub Paper Trick

Effect: Your friends will think that this is a Devil of a trick if you do it well. Pass a length of rope and a stiff piece of paper in the shape of a bell to your audience for examination. Next, have someone thread the bell onto the rope and then have him tie each end of the rope to your wrists (*Illus. C23*).

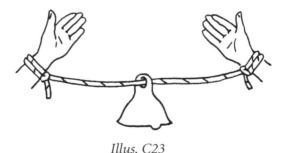

Illus. C23

You can even have him seal the knots with tape. Last, have him drape a large cloth over your arms so that your hands, the rope, and the bell are out of sight. In ten seconds flat, drop the cloth and show that the paper bell has been removed undamaged from the rope and that your hands are still securely tied. The rope and bell may once more be examined.

Materials Needed:
- One piece of rope three feet long
- Two identical paper bells
- A large cloth about three feet square

Preparation: Place one of the paper bells in your shirt pocket under your jacket.

Presentation: Everything occurs as described above up to the point where the cloth is placed over your arms. At this point, raise your arms chest high. Under cover of the cloth, tear the bell off the rope, crumple it up, and slip it into your inside jacket pocket. Remove the other paper bell from your shirt pocket and drop it on the table. Shake the cloth off your arms, and the trick is done. Another version of the trick would be to try secreting the second bell up the sleeve of your jacket instead of in your shirt pocket. This way, you wouldn't have to raise your arms up to your chest.

A Paper Magnet

Effect: "Yes, Ladies and Gentlemen, you heard me correctly: a paper magnet is both a possibility and a fact! Watch closely while I demonstrate this new wonder of science. First, I take this pencil and draw a picture of a magnet on this small piece of cardboard *(Illus. C24)*. Next, I cut a 2-inch piece from this paper straw and place it on the table. To magnetize the paper magnet, I rub it vigorously back and forth on a piece of cloth to build up a charge of static electricity.

"I now place the magnet on the table just in front of the paper straw. Watch this: As I move the magnet away from the straw, the straw follows it. Did you see that? Here, I'll do it once more before the magnet loses its power. There goes the straw again. It's amazing what new discoveries are made in science every day."

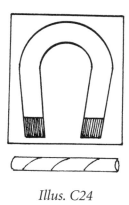

Illus. C24

Materials Needed:
- A pencil
- One small piece of cardboard
- A paper straw
- A piece of cloth

Presentation: The cardboard magnet isn't really magnetized. When the performer bends over the table and draws the card away from the straw, he opens his lips slightly and gently blows a stream of air down onto the table just behind the straw *(Illus. C25)*. A little practice will show you just how easy it is to make the piece of straw appear to be following the card across the table. You can also present this as a puzzle and see how long it takes your audience to discover how you make the straw move.

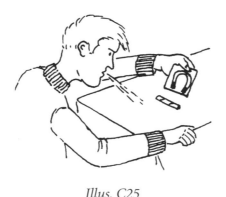

Illus. C25

Try not to purse your lips when you blow down on the table, as this can give the secret away. Just part your lips slightly when you blow on the straw. A steady flow of chatter and a lot of hand movement will help to distract your audience from seeing how you're really making the straw move.

The Heaven-and-Hell Paper Trick

This is a great bit of magic that can be done with a single sheet of paper. Present the following story to your audience.

"I once heard a story concerning greed that I would like to pass on to you. It seems that two souls confronted St. Peter at the gates of Heaven and asked to come in. St. Peter told them that there was but room for one of them and that they must therefore draw lots to see who was the worthier. St. Peter then took a sheet of paper and folded it once, and then once again, and finally a third time. (*Illus. C26–C29*).

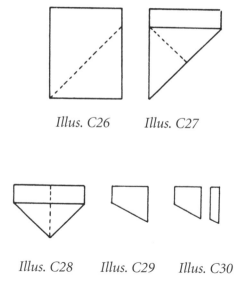

Illus. C26   *Illus. C27*

Illus. C28   *Illus. C29*   *Illus. C30*

He then tore the folded sheet of paper into two unequal portions *(Illus. C30)* and was about to speak when one of the two souls knocked the other aside and reached out and grabbed the larger portion of paper. 'I have the bigger piece,' he shouted. 'I won, let me in!"

"'Quiet,' commanded St. Peter, 'let us see what these lots have to tell us. The smaller piece belongs to this gentleman who has yet to speak. If we open it up, we find that it is in the shape of a cross *(Illus. 31)*. Now, let me have the piece that you so rudely took from me. Before we open it up, we will tear it down the middle *(Illus. C32)*. Now, we'll open up the pieces and see what they have to tell you.'

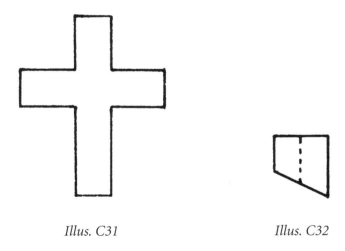

Illus. C31   *Illus. C32*

Illus. C33

"When the pieces were opened up, the hasty man found that they formed the word HELL *(Illus. C33)*.

"Seeing his fate clearly written before him the man turned to go, but St. Peter bade him enter along with the other man, saying, 'There is always room for one more up here, and I can see from this lesson that greed has been driven out of your heart for good.' I'd say that's a pretty good lesson for all of us."

The Fantastic Fir Tree

Effect: Take five or six sheets of newspaper and roll them into a tight tube while telling your audience a few jokes to keep their attention. At the conclusion of the jokes, turn this tube into a six-foot-high fir tree.

Materials Needed:
- Five or six strips of newspaper twelve inches in width, cut from several double-sheets of newspaper
- A rubber band

Presentation: Take one of the strips and start rolling it up into a cylinder. When you get to the last 5 inches of the strip, overlap another sheet *(Illus. C34)* and keep on rolling. Do this with each of the remaining sheets until the tube is complete.

Snap a rubber band around the tube near the bottom. Flatten out the tube and tear it down the center. Stop about two-thirds of the way down *(Illus. C35)*.

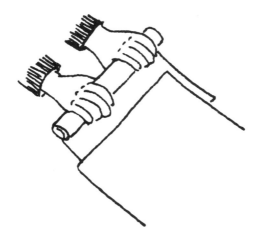

Illus. C34

Illus. C35

Flatten out the tube on the other side and tear it again the same way *(Illus. C36)*. Bend the four sections of strips down along the sides of the tube *(Illus. C37)*.

Take hold of the tube with one hand, and with the other reach into the center of the tube and take hold of a few of the strips. Gently pull them up and out of the tube. Keep pulling and working the strips upward *(Illus. C38)*.

You will end up with a paper fir tree about five or six feet high, depending on how many strips of paper you used to make the tube.

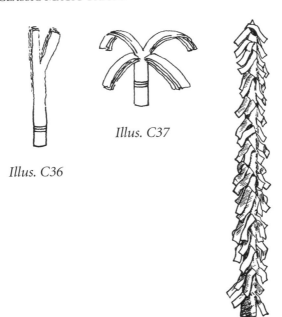

Illus. C36

Illus. C37

Illus. C38

MAGIC STRINGS & KNOTS

String, cord, rope, or rubber bands are usually readily available. The tricks in this section can provide impromptu merriment.

String Out #1

Required is a length of string or cord about 4' (1.2 m) long. Tie the ends in a square knot. Stick your thumbs inside the loop and extend the string. Display the string at about neck level for all to see.

"Now here's a real riddle for you: Do I have a magic neck or a magic string? I'll let you decide."

Without removing your thumbs, swing the looped string over your head so that the string is behind your neck *(Illus. C39)*.

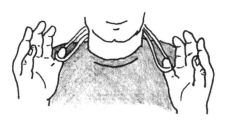

Illus. C39

For clarity, the string in all the string tricks is shown as thicker than it actually is.

Illus. C40

"Now watch carefully."

Quickly bring your hands together and insert your left first finger into the loop just behind your right thumb. Pull to the right with your right thumb and pull to the left with your left first finger. *Illus. C40* shows the beginning of this movement. Your left thumb naturally drops out of the loop, but only momentarily. Immediately, and without halting the motion, place your left thumb next to your left first finger and let the thumb take over the pulling motion to the left. Your left first finger will automatically be disengaged from the loop. Snap your thumbs against the inside of the loop as you extend the string forward. The position now is the same as at the beginning. Apparently, you've pulled the string through your neck!

The entire move is done in a fraction of a second. After you've practiced it a half-dozen times, you'll have mastered it for life.

If you feel like it, you could perform the stunt just one more time.

Note: The trick may be done in other ways. You may, for example, pull the string through a belt loop. Most effective, perhaps, is to place the string around a spectator's arm and then, apparently, pull it right through his arm.

String Out #2

With the same looped string from the previous trick, you can perform another escape.

Hold the string between your two hands, fingers pointed toward yourself *(Illus. C41)*. Bring the right side of the string over the left side, forming a small loop inside the larger loop *(Illus. C42)*. Between your teeth, lightly hold the portion where the strings cross.

Stick your left thumb into the end of the large loop, pulling it fairly tight, so that the smaller loop will be below it. Now, *from below,* stick your right first finger up through the smaller loop. Bring that finger over the right side of the large loop, under the left side, and to your nose. The dark arrow in *(Illus. C43)* shows the route of your first finger to your nose. Continue holding your right finger to the tip of your nose as you pull the larger loop with your left thumb and release the string from your teeth. The string comes free, apparently passing right through your fingers.

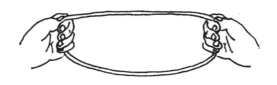

Illus. C41

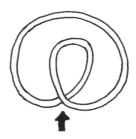

Grip with teeth here.

Illus. C42

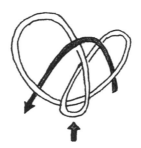

Grip with teeth here.

Illus. C43

No Noose Is Good Noose

You can perform yet another unusual escape trick with that same looped string or cord.

"Here we have an enormous noose," you say, placing the loop over your head. At about the halfway point, cross the loop in front of your face and grip the crossing point between your teeth.

As clearly as you can under these adverse circumstances, say, "But this would be a much more effective hanging device if it were a *double* noose."

Cross the cord back again *the same way,* and place the rest of the loop back over your head. If you originally crossed the right-hand portion on top, it's vital that you recross it on top.

Mumble dramatically and indistinguishably about what a thrilling climax this wonderful trick will have. Grip the string on the right side with your right hand, open your mouth, and quickly pull the string off.

The Sliding Knot

A stage magician cuts a length of rope into two pieces and ties two of the ends together. A spectator holds the loose ends. The magician grasps the knot in the middle and *slides it right off the rope,* and the rope is completely restored!

I've always found this effect to be both amazing and amusing. Here's a version you can do with a pair of scissors and a 3' (1 m) length of string or cord.

Tie the ends of the cord together, forming a loop. Hold this loop between your hands, fingers pointed toward yourself. (See *Illus. C41* on page 148 for the proper position.) Now, revolve your left hand, turning the string and forming a double loop. This is what spectators will assume you're doing. But in performance, you're much sneakier. When you form that double loop, you give the string an extra half-turn with your left hand. Thus, when you stretch out the double loop, a portion of the string is interlocked, as shown in *Illus. C44*. Naturally, you don't want spectators to see this interlocked portion. So, as you double the loop, quickly slide your right hand along the doubled string and conceal the interlock.

Move your left hand to within a few inches (cm) of your right, so that you're offering a small length of string for Craig, a helpful spectator, to cut with the scissors *(Illus. C45)*. You very wisely handed Craig the scissors before you started playing with the string. Invariably, your helper will cut at about the middle of the portion offered.

Illus. C44

Double-loop concealed here.

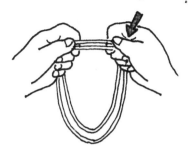

Illus. C45

Hold up the string in your right hand, demonstrating that it's in two pieces. Making sure you keep the interlock concealed with your right fingers, carefully tie the ends of the small piece into a square knot. Now you need no longer conceal anything.

Ask Craig to hold the two loose ends of the string. Make some mystical waves over the string, mumbling some magic words. Look a little disappointed. Try again. You're even more disappointed. "The magic doesn't seem to be working," you tell Craig. "But I'd like to give you a little something for helping out. I *know* you won't take money, so what can I give you? I've got it!" Slide the knot along the string, moving his hand to one side as you remove the knot from the string. Present him with the knot. Hold up the string by the ends. "Say! That *is* sort of magic."

And Slide Again

Using (about) a 3' (1 m) piece of string or cord, you might try this trick, which is about as easy as magic ever gets.

Hold the string at one end and let it hang down. Ask Donna to point out the middle of the string. Take one end and tie it to the string at that point *(Illus. C46)*.

Illus. C46

Make sure you keep track of the portion leading to the knot, which is darkened in the illustration. Ask Donna to cut the "middle of the string." Actually have her cut at the point indicated by the arrow in *Illus. C46*. Do so by holding the string between your hands and presenting only this portion to her.

Ask Donna to hold both ends of the string. You can now slide off the knot and present it to her, as you did in the previous trick. The following, however, might be a better conclusion. Hold the knot in your right fist. Bring your left hand over, apparently to take the knot. Actually, your left hand grips the point where the knot was, while your right hand slides the knot to your right. As you continue sliding the knot to the end of the string, say, "Could you pull the string a little tighter?" Move her hand aside with yours. She regrips the string, and you slide the knot off.

You can casually put your right hand in your pocket and leave the knot there as you massage the string with your left hand, restoring it. Or you can go to your pocket for *magic dust*, leaving the knot there. The invisible *magic dust* is sprinkled over your left hand, bringing about the restoration of the string.

The Incredible Knot

G. W. Hunter invented this clever trick. You can use a 3' (1 m) length of string, cord, or rope.

You ask, "The question is, 'Can anyone tie a knot in a string without letting of the ends?' The answer is no, unless you happen to be magical, a no-good sneak, or a lowdown rascal. And since I'm two out of three of those, I'll give it a try. Watch closely as I tie a knot without letting go of the ends."

Hold the string between your hands, as shown *(Illus. C47)*.

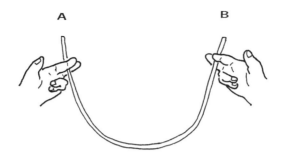

For convenience the string is shown as shorter than it actually is.

Illus. C47

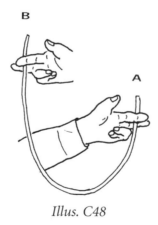

Illus. C48

Bring end B over your left wrist (*Illus. C48*) and around the back of your left hand to the position shown in *Illus. C49*. Bring end B through the loop, as shown by the dark arrow in Illus. 11. Do not let go of end B.

Say, "I've done nothing underhanded—well, I have done something underhanded and (actually) overhanded—but nothing you haven't seen. The ends haven't left my fingers, yet the knot is already formed. But I do *not* use sleight of hand; I use *magic*. To prove it, I'm not going to do anything fast, or switch the ends, or do anything else sneaky." Address Mike, a spectator, "I want you to take one end in each hand and pull." When he does, a knot will form in the middle of the string.

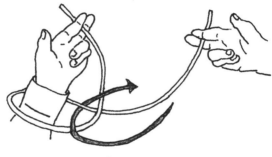

Illus. C49

Knot at All

Here's a simple, effective follow-up to the two preceding tricks.

Invite Martin and Wally to help out. Take the ends of your 3' (1 m) string in your hands, about 5" (13 cm) from the ends. Cross the right-hand section in front of the left (as you look at it) and grip the intersection between your left thumb and fingers. Pull End A through the loop *(Illus. C50)*. Pull End A to the right for several inches (cms) and then hand the end to Martin, asking him to hold that end for a moment.

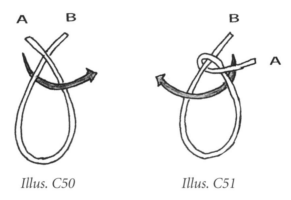

Illus. C50   *Illus. C51*

Transfer the intersecting point (now a knot, but only briefly) to your right hand, so that you're now holding the point between your right thumb and fingers. Put End B through the loop, as indicated by the arrow shown in *(Illus. C51)*. Pull End B to the left for several inches, and hand that end to Wally.

Still covering the "knot" with your right hand, ask Martin and Wally to pull on the string. When the string is taut, say, "Whoa! You pulled too hard. The knot popped right off." Remove your right hand from the string and toss the invisible knot into the air. Invite them to examine the string—the knot's gone!

Or Knot to Be

Similar in *effect* to the preceding trick, this may well be the easiest method to cause a "knot" to disappear.

Take the ends of a 3' (1 m) string and tie them together. Hold the loop in your hands, as shown in *Illus. C41*, on page 148. Make sure that your right hand covers the knot.

Give the loop one complete twist *(Illus. C52)*.

Grasp here.

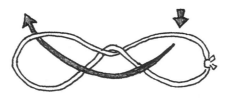

Illus. C52

This, in effect, divides the string into two loops. With your left hand, reach past the point where the string crosses, grasp one of the strands, and pull the strand through the loop on the left. The dark arrow in *Illus. C52* shows this process. Pull the ends so that a knot forms in the middle. One of the strands (probably the top one) will slide through the knot. Say, "We'd better tighten the knot." Cover the knot with your left hand and pull on the appropriate strand with your right hand, sliding the knot to the left. When the knot is quite small, grip it tightly between your left thumb and left first finger. Jerk the strand with your right hand, pretending to tighten the knot. Actually, of course, the so-called knot can vanish by simply holding the string on either side of the knot and pulling on the other side. Go to the actual knot and, in similar fashion, tighten it. "Might as well tighten this one, too."

Go back to the false knot and grip it lightly between your left thumb and left first finger; your other fingers grip the string. "I need a lot more fibre in my diet. This could be a start." With your right hand, grasp the same strand it held before and pull the strand tight, popping the knot out of the string. At the same time, with your left hand, apparently pick off the knot and pop it into your mouth. As you chew and swallow, display the string, showing that the knot's gone.

Eye of the Needle

There's no particular relationship between the simplicity of a trick and the audience reaction. Here's a good example. The trick itself is very easy to perform, but the audience is usually astonished. What's more, because the result seems so impossible, *you'll* be delightfully surprised every time you perform it. To achieve this wonderful result, however, you must follow the instructions carefully.

You'll need a 3' (1 m) length of cord or string. Ask, "Has anyone here ever tried to thread a needle?" After the response, continue, "Well, I find it almost impossible. In fact, the *only* way I can do it is by resorting to magic. Let me show you what I mean."

Grasp the string about 8" (20 cm) from the bottom and wrap it around your thumb in a clockwise direction at least a half-dozen times. The string should be wrapped fairly loosely. Form a loop in the string, holding it between your left thumb and your left first finger *(Illus. C53)*.

Illus. C53

Display the loop, saying, "This is the eye of the needle." With your right fingers and thumb, grasp the 8" (20 cm) length of string you let hang loose at the beginning. Hold it a few inches (cms) from the end. "This is the thread. You can see that the eye of this particular needle is enormous. Even so, I'll probably have difficulty threading it. But to make it even more difficult, I'll try to thread the needle—*without letting go of the thread.* Clearly, this calls for magic. So let me try my magic words:

Maybe my outstanding speed'll
Help me push this through the needle.

Now it's time for some great acting. With a quick forward movement, try to push the "thread" through the eye. Failure! Repeat the magic words and try again. Another failure! Again the magic words, and yet *another* failure. Say the magic words with great emphasis, and you'll finally succeed. Well, not actually. On your last attempt, brush the bottom of the loop with the bottom of your right hand, and then pull the string sharply upwards, letting a loop slip off your left thumb. It indeed looks as though you threaded the needle without letting go of the "thread."

Say, "It worked! So next time you want to thread a needle, try to remember the magic words."

As you'll discover, it takes some experimentation to get the moves exactly right, but the result is well worth the effort.

Candy Is Dandy

This is a trick in which you reveal the "secret" at the end. If you prefer, you could eliminate the last part and do the trick as straight magic.

All you need for this trick is a length of string, a handkerchief, and a roll of multicolored hole-in-the-middle candy.

In your right pocket you have a length of string and a candy, preferably light-colored. In your left pocket, you have a *bright-colored* candy at the bottom and a folded handkerchief well above it. On top of all this, you have a piece of candy which is the same color as the candy you have in your right pocket.

Reach into your right pocket and take out the candy and the string. Hold up the candy for all to see. Run the string through the hole, and then run one end of the string through the hole again so that the candy is held at the bottom of a loose loop *(Illus. C53a)*.

Illus. C53a

This is done as misdirection; spectators might feel that there's something tricky about the way the candy is held on the string.

Get two spectators to hold the ends of the string. Reach into your left pocket. Grip the candy in your loosely curled fingers. Grasp a corner of the handkerchief between your first finger and thumb and pull the cloth from your pocket, snapping it open. Use both hands to lay the handkerchief over the string, concealing the candy that's hanging there.

Take the candy from your left hand into your right. Chat fairly loudly about the difficulty of the feat you're trying to perform; you're trying to cover any noise you might make as you break the candy that's hanging on the string. Make as clean a break as you can, because you don't want to deal with too many little pieces. Hold these pieces in your curled left fingers.

Hold the unbroken candy between your right fingertips and your right thumb. Drop your left hand down so that you can grasp an edge of the handkerchief between your first finger and your thumb. Whip the handkerchief off the string, and, with your right hand, hold up the candy for all to see.

Immediately, place the handkerchief into your left pocket. Shove the pieces of candy to the bottom of your left pocket. Grasp the multicolored candy and rest it on top of the handkerchief. Remove your hand from your pocket.

As you produce the liberated candy, some spectators may see through the trick. Don't let them analyze. Instantly say, "Don't say a word. I know exactly what you're thinking. Can he possibly do that again? Of course I can."

Quickly thread the candy onto the string, exactly as before. Have your assistants hold the ends of the string. Reach into your left pocket and take the bright-colored candy into your curled fingers. Grip the handkerchief between your thumb and your first finger and pull the handkerchief from your pocket. Be careful that you don't bring out any broken candy pieces along with the handkerchief. Proceed exactly as before. The broken pieces go into your left pocket, along with the handkerchief, and the liberated candy is held up for all to see.

There's one little problem: It's a different color! Stare at it for a moment in apparent shock. Say, "Oh-oh!" Pause briefly. Then say, "Real magic, ladies and gentlemen. Not only have I removed the candy from the string, but I've magically caused it to change color."

Join in the general merriment. Sometimes a few of the less astute in your audience will wonder what all the laughter is about.

RUBBER BAND MAGIC

A Bouncy Band

For this amusing stunt, you'll need two rubber bands.

Say, "Some people tie a piece of string around their finger to remind them of something. I use a rubber band. For example, I was supposed to buy one or two loaves of bread, so I put a rubber band around my first and second fingers." Place one rubber band over the first two fingers of your right hand, displaying it as shown (*Illus. C54—your view*). Holding the back of your right hand toward the onlookers, pull back the rubber band, using your left hand. Close the fingers of your right hand, so that when you release with your left hand, the rubber band will be outside all of your fingers (*Illus. C55*).

Illus. C54   *Illus. C55*

"Unfortunately, rubber bands aren't very reliable, so when I go to the store…" Straighten up your right-hand fingers. The rubber band will jump over, so that it will surround the other two fingers. "…the rubber band was on my third and fourth fingers. So I bought four loaves of bread."

Repeat the stunt, saying, "This kept happening to me every time I went to the store."

The feat you're about to perform is actually no more difficult than your first stunt, but it seems to be miraculous. "One day I decided to trap the rubber band so that it couldn't switch fingers on me."

Place the rubber band over the first two fingers of your right hand, as you did before. Pick up the other rubber band with your left hand and wrap it around the fingers of your right hand.

Illus. C56

"But when I got to the store…" Follow the exact same procedure as before, and the rubber band will once again jump over so that it encircles the other two fingers. Shrug. "Again, four loaves of bread." Shake your head. "It didn't matter. I was supposed to buy *milk* anyway."

That Band Really Jumps

It's always fun to involve a spectator in a funny bit of by-play. Ruth is supposed to have a great sense of humor; let's test it.

Place a rubber band on the first finger of your left hand, letting the band hang down *(Illus. C57)*.

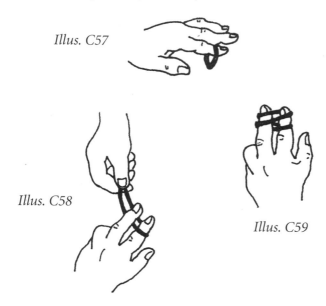

Illus. C57

Illus. C58

Illus. C59

Bring the band under your middle finger *(Illus. C58)*, and then over the top of your middle finger. Hook the end of the band onto the tip of your first finger. *Illus. C59* shows a simplified view of the final position. The rubber band should be at the very end of your fingers, attached between the first joint and the tip.

Hold your left hand upright, and ask Ruth to hold the tip of your first finger and end up around your middle finger.

Now it's time to display your performance skills. Stare at the rubber band with a puzzled look. Frown at Ruth. "I thought I asked you to hold my first finger. Let's try again."

Repeat the whole routine, admonishing Ruth, "Now would you *please* hold on?" By the third time, she should really be squeezing the tip of your first finger. You might complain in mock seriousness, "Ow! That's tight enough."

You should probably quit after three or four tries, thanking Ruth for giving it a try. "After all, you did your best. It's probably not all your fault that it didn't work out."

ROPE 'EM IN

The Hindu Bangle Trick

Effect: From the fabled regions of the Indian subcontinent comes the Hindu Bangle Trick, which, when performed well, is truly amazing. Follow closely the details of its presentation.

Ask someone to come forward from the audience to assist you. Hand him a stout length of rope, about two and a half feet in length, and have him tie both ends of the rope to your wrists *(Illus. C60)*.

The knots should be very tight and even sealed with tape to heighten the effect.

Next, hand your assistant a plastic ring some 4" in diameter. Instruct him to pass it among the audience to verify that it is not a trick ring nor has it been tampered with in any way. When he returns the ring to you, instruct him to drape a three-foot-square cloth over your hands and arms. Then tell him to step back and slowly count to five, let the cloth slip to the floor; the audience will see that the ring is now threaded on the rope. On examination, your wrists are found to be securely bound *(Illus. C61)*.

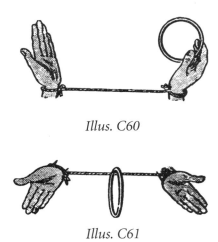

Illus. C60

Illus. C61

Instruct your assistant to cut you free, and step back to acknowledge the thunderous applause.

Materials Needed:
- Two matching bangles
- A three-foot-square cloth
- A stout, two-and-a-half-foot length of rope

Presentation: How is this trick accomplished? Buy two matching bangles. When you present this trick, the second one is already on your arm, halfway up your sleeve. Under cover of the cloth, slip your hand up your sleeve and bring the bangle down. Hold this bangle with one hand while slipping the first bangle (the one you showed to the audience) with your other hand onto a hook inside your coat. Or slip the ring back up the sleeve of your coat and get rid of it as soon as possible.

Here, There, Everywhere

Effect: All that is needed to perform this rope trick is a four-foot length of rope and an eight-inch-diameter wooden embroidery ring. (Any large, solid ring will do.) Pick up a piece of rope and show it to the audience. There are three knots tied in the rope. The solid wooden ring hangs on one of the end knots *(Illus. C62)*.

Illus. C62

Illus. C63

Illus. C64

Pass the rope behind your back, and the ring will jump to the knot at the other end of the rope *(Illus. C63)*. Once again pass the rope behind your back, and the ring jumps back to the other end *(Illus. C62)*. The third time you do this, however, the ring is found to have jumped to the middle knot *(Illus. C64)*. Immediately hand the rope, with the ring still securely tied to the middle knot, out for inspection.

The secret lies in the fact that there is a fourth knot tied in the rope. This knot is hidden by your hand, which covers the knot when you hold the rope *(Illus. C65)*. Also, the bottom knot on the rope is a slip knot *(Illus. C66)*.

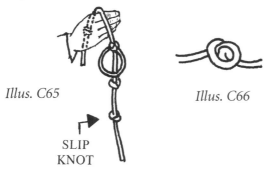

Illus. C65

SLIP
KNOT

Illus. C66

Presentation: Pick up the rope with your right hand, remembering to conceal the extra knot *(Illus. C65)* and hold it up to the audience *(Illus. C62)*. When you pass the rope behind your back, cover the end with the extra knot with your left hand. Then show the rope to the audience *(Illus. C63)*. The previous action is reversed for the next pass. During the final pass behind your back, pull the rope tight so that slip knot will come apart and disappear. Now bring the rope out. The ring will be on the middle knot. A perfect deception.

A Knotty Problem

Effect: Stand before the audience and ask: "Did you ever have one of those days where everything seems to go wrong? Of course you have. The other day I was practicing tying some knots while I was working on a new escape trick. First, I tied a reef knot like this one, but when I pulled it tight it just disappeared. See, the same thing has happened with this knot.

"Next, I tried tying a Bulgarian Shoelace Knot, but when I went to pull it tight, it too disappeared just like this.

"Luckily, when I tried to tie a knot without letting go of either end, my magic powers returned and I succeeded" (at this point, use the *Impossible Knot,* page 175).

Materials Needed:
- One three-foot length of soft rope

Presentation: Let's start with the first knot to disappear, the Reef Knot. Just follow the instructions in *Illus. C67–C69*. When the knot is made it looks formidable, but it will melt away like butter when you pull the ends apart.

The Bulgarian Shoelace Knot takes a bit more description. Place the rope over your hands as shown in *Illus. C70*. Clip the two loops between the first and second fingers of each hand and pull your hands apart *(Illus. C71)*. Pull the rope tight and you will have formed a shoelace knot. Next, reach through the right-hand loop with the thumb and first finger of your right hand and grasp end B of the rope *(Illus. C72)*.

FIRST TIE A
REEF KNOT
LIKE THIS:

Illus. C67

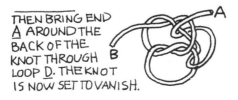

THEN BRING END
A AROUND THE
BACK OF THE
KNOT THROUGH
LOOP D. THE KNOT
IS NOW SET TO VANISH.

Illus. C68

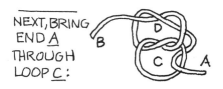

NEXT, BRING END <u>A</u> THROUGH LOOP <u>C</u>:

Illus. C69

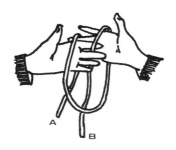

Illus. C70

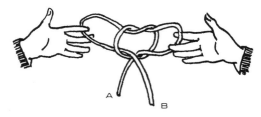

Illus. C71

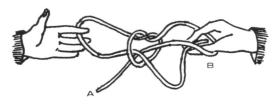

Illus. C72

Do the same with your left hand, grasping end A. Pull the ends through the loops *(Illus. C73)* and pull the rope tight, forming a knot in the middle *(Illus. C74).* Pause a moment and then pull hard on the two ends. The knot will disappear in the twinkling of an eye *(Illus. C75).*

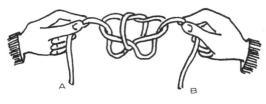

Illus. C73

Illus. C74

Illus. C75

This presentation, in which you have failed to tie two different knots, is a perfect lead-in to the *Impossible Knot*.

Impossible Knot

Effect: Challenge someone in the audience to come forward and tie a knot in a three-foot length of rope without letting go of either end of the rope. After he has made a few unsuccessful attempts, take the rope from him and proceed to show how it can be done three different ways. This is a trick that violates the axiom of never showing the same trick more than once to the same audience.

Materials Needed:
- A three-foot length of the soft rope
- Transparent tape

Presentation: For the first method of tying, place the rope on a tabletop. Fold your arms in front of your chest and bend over the table. With your left hand, reach under your right arm and pick up the right end of the rope. With your right hand, reach over your left arm and pick up the left end of the rope.

Now, unfold your arms, drawing them apart. Stretch them far apart, and a knot will be formed in the center of the rope. This is method one.

For the second method, pick up the rope in both hands as shown in *Illus. C76*. Now, loop the rope over and behind your left wrist as shown in *Illus. C77*.

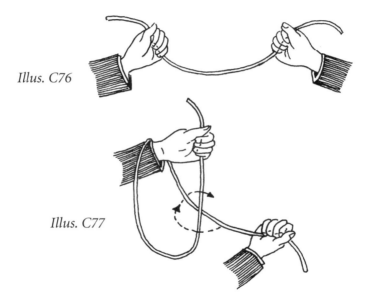

Illus. C76

Illus. C77

Continue looping by weaving the end around the back strand as shown in *Illus. C77* and *C78*. When you're finished, your hands, palms up, should look like the hands shown in *Illus. C79*.

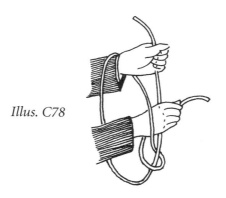

Illus. C78

Illus. C79

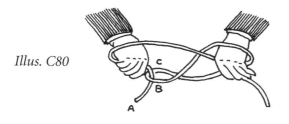

Illus. C80

Now comes the important move of the trick. Turn both palms down, letting the loops slide off the back of your hands. However, when you do this your right hand should let go of rope end A and grasp the rope at point C. As the loops slide off your hands, rope end A slides through loop B; this allows you to stretch your arms apart, thus forming a knot in the center of the rope *(Illus. C80)*. The action is so fast that the audience cannot see you releasing and then regrasping the end of the rope.

At this point, pause and pretend to see a look of doubt in one or two faces in the audience. Then say, "I think that one or two of you are still not convinced that I can indeed tie a knot in a rope without letting go of either end. Very well, I will show you once again, but this time I will do it under test conditions!"

Now have the gentleman who first assisted you take the transparent tape and firmly tape each end of the rope to your first fingers *(Illus. C81)*.

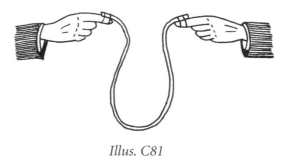

Illus. C81

When this is done, repeat the previous steps up through and including *Illus. C79*. At this point say, "I have just completed the knot, but you cannot see it. To prove it, I want this gentleman to remove the ends of the rope from my fingers and to then stretch the rope apart. There, you see! There is a knot in the middle just as I said there would be. I've shown you how to do this feat three different ways. Now go home and entertain your friends with this amazing bit of rope magic!"

The Impossible Linking Ropes

Effect: You, the magician, will perform the seemingly impossible task of linking together two pieces of rope while they are hidden under a handkerchief.

Materials Needed:
- Two three-foot lengths of rope. One rope is white, and the other is dyed red.
- One heavy pocket handkerchief.

Presentation: Place the two lengths of rope on the table in front of you. Loop each rope in the form of a U and place them side by side as shown in *Illus. C82*. The loop ends should be toward you.

Illus. C82

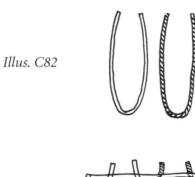

Illus. C83

Illus. C84

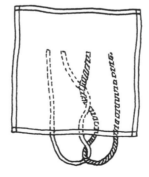

Next, open up a heavy white pocket handkerchief and drape it over the two ropes, leaving the ends exposed *(Illus. C83)*. Now, reach under the handkerchief and tell your audience that you are causing the ropes to link together. What you are doing is to pull one side of the red rope over the nearer side of the white rope, and then to tuck the red rope back under, as shown in *Illus. C83*.

A moment later, bring your hands out and take hold of the bottom ends of the handkerchief. Then draw the handkerchief away from you until the linked loops of the rope came into view *(Illus. C84)*. Keep moving the cloth down until the ends of the rope are covered.

Move your hands back to the top of the cloth, and then pick up the two linked ropes and the handkerchief as one and hold it up in front of you *(Illus. C85)*. At this point the cords will untangle themselves automatically behind the cloth. After three or four seconds, let the handkerchief drop to the table. Lay the two linked ropes down on the table in front of you and elaborate on the impossibility that the audience has just witnessed.

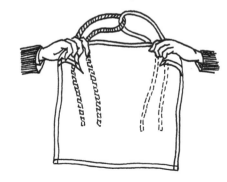

Illus. C85

Perfect Rope Trick

Effect: To the audience, this will seem to be truly an "impossible" rope trick. Display three pieces of rope, all of different lengths. Then cause the shortest piece to grow in length and the longest piece to shrink until all the pieces are of the same length. After showing each piece to the audience, cause the pieces of rope to return to their original lengths. Then immediately pass out the three pieces for examination.

Materials Needed:
- Three pieces of rope. The short piece should be 12" long, the medium piece 28", and the long piece 42".

Presentation: Hold up the short piece of rope and place it in your left hand. Next, exhibit the long piece and place this in your left hand. Last, show the medium piece and place this too in your left hand *(Illus. C86)*. Keep the back of your left hand turned toward the audience.

Bring the end of the medium-length rope up so that it is next to its other end. Then bring the end of the short piece up and cross it over the end of the long piece that is held in your left hand. Finally, bring the end of the long piece up and over the loop of the short piece *(Illus. C87)*.

Now you are ready to cause all of the ropes to assume the same length. Reach over with your right hand and take hold of one end of the medium-length rope, the end to the right. Also, take hold

of the two ends of the long rope. Your left hand is now holding the left end of the medium-length rope and both ends of the short-length rope. At this point, the short rope and the long rope are looped together. This is hidden from the audience by the back of the left hand.

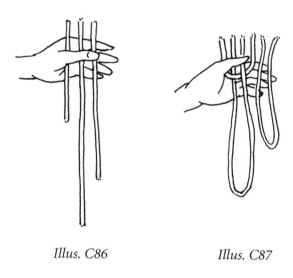

Illus. C86   *Illus. C87*

Grip the ropes tightly with both hands and start to move your hands apart *(Illus. C88)*. Keep moving your hands apart until the ropes appear to be the same length *(Illus. C89)*. Let go of the ends in your right hand. You are now holding the three ropes in your left hand, and they all appear to be of the same length.

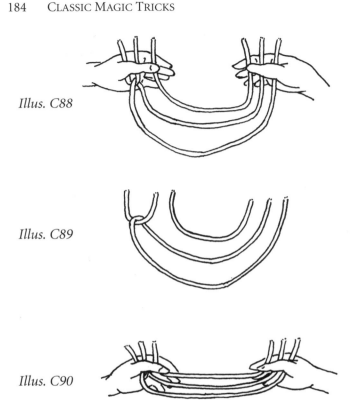

Illus. C88

Illus. C89

Illus. C90

At this point, count the ropes, apparently showing each one of them individually. First, reach over and take hold of the medium length of rope and pull it away from your left hand *(Illus. C90)*. Count, "One!"

Then bring your right hand back to get the second rope. What you are actually doing is taking the two ends of the short rope in your right thumb and forefinger and clipping the medium-length rope with the forefinger and index finger of your left hand *(Illus. C91)*. When you move your hands apart, you are holding the looped short and long pieces in your right hand and the medium piece in your left hand *(Illus. C92)*. To the audience it will appear that you placed a second piece of rope into your right hand. Count aloud, "Two!" Through all of this the loop between the two ropes is concealed by both your left and right hands. Both are at all times turned toward the audience.

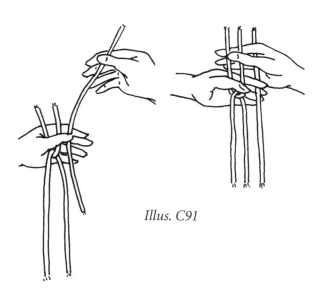

Illus. C91

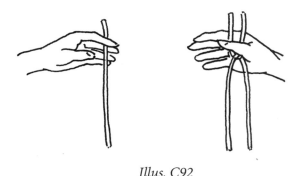

Illus. C92

Finally, move your right hand back and use it to draw the medium-length rope through the fingers of your left hand *(Illus. C93)*. Count aloud, "Three!"

At this point, you have caused the three ropes to become equal in length. To finish the trick, you now have to make them return to their original lengths. Transfer the ropes from your right hand to your left hand *(Illus. C94)*. Make sure that the loop is not seen.

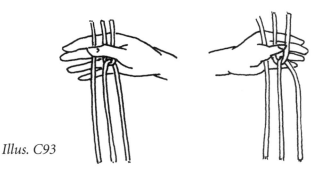

Illus. C93   *Illus. C94*

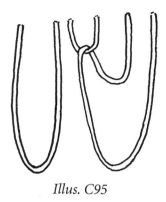

Illus. C95

Take the dangling ends of the ropes, one by one, and position them in your left hand, as shown in *Illus. C95*. The ends of each rope should end up being side-by-side in your hand. Now, slowly take hold of one of the ends of the short rope and pull on it until the short rope comes free from your left hand. Make sure that the loop is not drawn up into view. Toss the rope to the audience. Next, draw the medium-length rope from your hand and toss it to the audience. Finally, display the long rope and pass it out for examination.

Thus ends the perfect rope trick. There are no "extra" pieces to dispose of; the ropes are genuine, and everything can be examined once the trick is concluded.

PROPS, EFFECTS, & ILLUSIONS

WHAT THE EYE CAN'T SEE

Glass-Through-the-Table Bafflement

Effect: You cover a coin on a table with a glass, wrapped in paper or a stiff napkin. You ask the spectators to use their powers of concentration to flip the coin over. When it doesn't seem to work, you smash down on the covered glass in frustration, then produce it intact from under the table. This is an old but very effective trick that catches everyone by surprise due to the misdirection of attention to the idea of turning a coin over with mind power.

Materials Needed:
- Table covered with a tablecloth
- Heavy water glass
- Square of newspaper or a stiff napkin
- Silver quarter

Presentation: Sit behind a covered table, place a coin on it and remark: "I am now going to show you an experiment in Mind over Matter! Note that this coin is heads up on the table."

You then place an inverted water glass over the coin and cover the glass with a sheet of newspaper or a stiffly starched napkin, wrapped in a cone. Say, "I want everyone to concentrate on the coin and visualize it turning over on the table. Very good! Your minds are very strong. I think that the coin is now tails up."

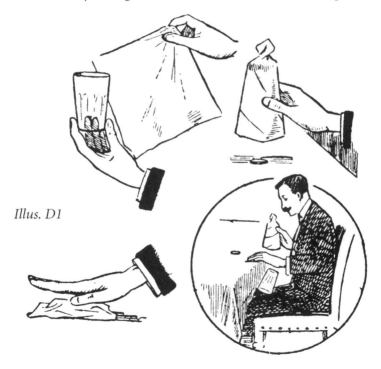

Illus. D1

You lift the cone and glass together in your left had. Everyone looks at the coin, which is still heads up. As you bend over the look at the coin, move the cone and glass back past the edge of the table and let the glass slide out and drop into your lap *(Illus. D1)*.

The top of the table will effectively hide this action. Without pausing more than a second, move the paper or cloth shell back over the coin. The stiff paper or cloth will retain its shape and look as though the glass is still under it. You continue:

"I guess I was wrong. Let's try it again." After a moment or two, exclaim, "This is never going to work! You're thinking about the glass, not the coin!" With that, smash your hand down on top of the cone, crumpling it to the table and making everyone jump in surprise. The glass has disappeared. While they are wondering where it went, reach under the table and pretend to catch the glass going through the bottom of the table. Bring it out saying, "Look! You caused the glass to go right through the table!"

Serfs-and-Sheep Scramble

Effect: Here's an entertaining old trick about two hungry serfs and a barn full of sheep. During each of the 16 moves a walnut is either placed in a hat or is removed from a hat to represent the action taking place.

Materials Needed:

- 2 hats to represent the Sheriff's two barns
- 7 walnuts; 5 to represent the sheep, 2 to represent the serfs

Presentation: According to the story, in the days of Robin Hood two hungry serfs wandered onto the estate of the Sheriff of Nottingham. The desperate men decided to steal the five sheep and kill them in the barns. Each serf selected a barn. (Place one walnut into each hat.) Follow the numbered diagrams following (*Illus. D2–D3*) to show how the story unfolds and the surprise ending.

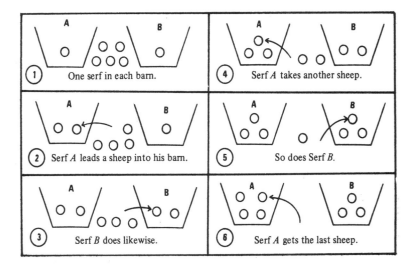

Illus. D2

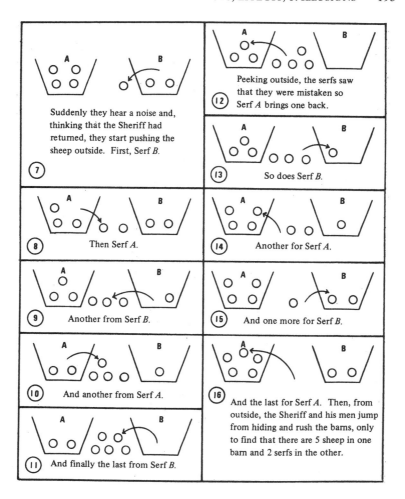

7. Suddenly they hear a noise and, thinking that the Sheriff had returned, they start pushing the sheep outside. First, Serf *B*.

8. Then Serf *A*.

9. Another from Serf *B*.

10. And another from Serf *A*.

11. And finally the last from Serf *B*.

12. Peeking outside, the serfs saw that they were mistaken so Serf *A* brings one back.

13. So does Serf *B*.

14. Another for Serf *A*.

15. And one more for Serf *B*.

16. And the last for Serf *A*. Then, from outside, the Sheriff and his men jump from hiding and rush the barns, only to find that there are 5 sheep in one barn and 2 serfs in the other.

Illus. D3

The Domino Mystery

Effect: Dump a box of dominoes and a sealed envelope on the table. Ask two members of the audience to set up the dominoes in a long line on the table, matching the ends of each domino as you would when playing a game. When they open up the envelope and read the paper, it has printed on it the two numbers at each end of the line.

Materials Needed:
- Dominoes
- Envelope
- Note paper
- Pencil

Preparation: If you were to lay out a complete set of dominoes in a circle, they would match where the two ends came together. Thus, if you remove any domino from the box and then lay them out in a straight line, the two end dominoes will always match the two numbers on the domino that you removed. Before showing this trick, you must remove the 2 : 4 domino from the box, write a note containing those two numbers, and seal the note in the envelope. Make sure no one gets to see that there is a domino missing from the box before you dump it out on the table.

Presentation: Dump the box (minus one) of dominoes and the sealed envelope on the table. Ask for two members of the audience to set up the dominoes in a long line on the table, matching the ends of each domino as you would when playing a game.

When they're finished, explain to them that prior to today's performance you had a mental picture of a long line of dominoes and that you jotted down the numbers on the two end dominoes and placed this information in the envelope that is on the table. Ask one of them to open the envelope and read what you wrote on the paper inside: "The number at one end of the line of dominoes is four, and the number at the other end is two."

The Balancing Glass Mystery

Effect: During an interlude at the dinner table, take a half-full glass of water and, with nonchalance, balance it on the edge of its base. After a minute or so, set it back on its base. The audience can now examine the glass and the tabletop for clues to the secret of this wonderful feat of juggling. Even if they look under the tablecloth, they will find nothing.

Materials Needed:
- Half-filled heavy water glass
- One-inch piece of match stick or toothpick
- Long piece of strong black thread

Preparation: The secret lies in the match stick. Beforehand, tie the end of the thread around the middle of the match stick *(Illus. D4)*. Place the match stick under the tablecloth in front of your place at the dinner table. The end of the string should hang down a couple of inches below the edge of the tablecloth. Since there is always the chance of someone trying this trick after you have presented it, and spilling water all over the table, it's best to present this stunt in your own home.

Illus. D4

Presentation: The match stick is small and will not be noticed in the folds and creases of the tablecloth. Wait until dessert and coffee to present this juggling sensation. Without mentioning what you're doing, take the glass and place it down so that its edge is resting on the wooden match. Now, adjust it until it's well balanced *(Illus. D5)*. By the time your fellow diners will see what you are doing, and you will amaze them with this glass-balancing feat.

When it comes time to right the glass, reach out with your right hand to grasp it. Your left hand should be below the table, holding the end of the black thread. When you grip the glass, raise it up slightly and move it forward so that your hand covers the spot where the match stick is positioned beneath the tablecloth.

While everyone's attention is on the glass, pull the match stick towards you. Your arm will cover the movement under the cloth. Keep pulling on the thread until the match stick is in your left hand. It is now safe to let your audience examine the glass and the tablecloth.

A slightly more elaborate method of doing this trick is to have a secret assistant at the table pull the thread for you. In this case, you can have both hands plainly in sight during the entire performance. It would be best if your accomplice were sitting directly across the table from you.

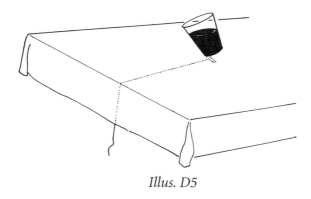

Illus. D5

Great Ribbon-and-Ring Mystery

Effect: Form a loop in the center of a length of ribbon and secure it with a safety pin. Then borrow a ring from someone and state that you will cause the ring to be placed on the loop without threading it through either end of the ribbon. Cover the loop and ring with a handkerchief, put your hands under the cloth, and seconds later remove the handkerchief, showing that the ring has become threaded on the center of the ribbon.

Materials Needed:
- Three-foot length of colored half-inch-wide ribbon
- Large safety pin
- Large handkerchief or scarf
- Finger ring

Presentation: Form a loop in the center of the ribbon and fasten it with a stout safety pin. Then place the borrowed finger ring next to it *(Illus. D6)*. Next, place a handkerchief over the loop and ring and reach under it with both hands. With your hands under the cloth, remove the safety pin, take the top of the loop, and thread it through the ring *(Illus. D7)*.

Illus. D6

Illus. D7

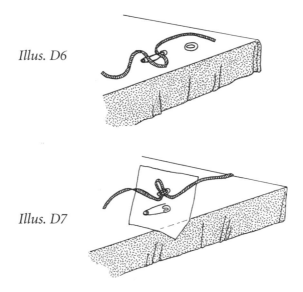

This forms two loops in the ribbon, one facing up and one facing down. Now, take the safety pin and fasten it through the two sides of the "down" loop on the left of the ring *(Illus. D8)*. Next, hook the little finger of your right hand through the "up" loop on the right side *(Illus. D9)* pinching the handkerchief from underneath between the thumb and first finger of that hand.

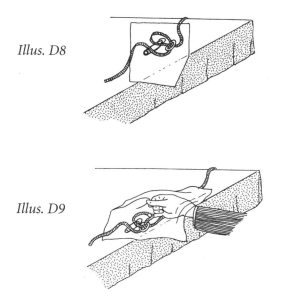

Illus. D8

Illus. D9

Now bring your left hand from under the cloth to the left end of the ribbon. Hold down that end of the ribbon with the fingers of your left hand. Make a smooth swiping motion to the right with your right hand, pulling the ribbon loop with your hooked little finger and dragging the handkerchief along the ribbon until it is clear of the table. If you make the motion quickly enough, the handkerchief should mask the flip of the ribbon as it pulls free.

The ribbon is now open to view on the table, with the ring neatly threaded in the center and firmly secured by the safety pin (*Illus. D10*).

Illus. D10

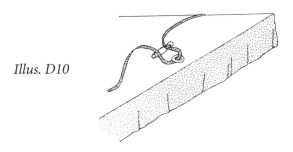

There are two important points to remember when presenting this trick. First, make sure that the ends of the ribbon are always in view on either side of the handkerchief. Tell your audience to watch the ends while your hands are under the cloth. Second, before removing the handkerchief from the ribbon, be sure that your left hand is holding down the left end of the ribbon firmly against the top of the table. If the end is not anchored, you will not be able to pull the loose end of the ribbon through the ring with the little finger of your right hand as you sweep the handkerchief to the right.

RIGGED GIMMICKS

The Pencil-and-String Perplexity

Effect: This is a clever trick that's sure to leave the audience perplexed. Show the audience a pencil that has a loop of string attached to it. Next, loop the pencil through the buttonhole in a spectator's shirt or coat. Once the pencil is in place, bet the spectator that he can't remove it in five minutes. Inform the spectator that he is not allowed to cut the string, break the pencil, or cut the buttonhole in attempting to win this bet.

Materials Needed:
- A stout piece of string about two feet long
- A new pencil

Preparation: This is an easy magic trick to perform. It is also inexpensive, so have pencils made up with your name on them to give away for advertising.

To do the trick, you must first drill a hole in the pencil below the eraser. Then thread the piece of string through the hole and tie it so that when pulled tight the loop is about an inch from the end of the pencil *(Illus. D11)*.

Illus. D11

Presentation: To loop the pencil on a buttonhole, first place the fingers of your right hand through the loop in the string. Then, take hold of the buttonhole with your right hand and pull it and the cloth around it through the loop of string. Pull it far enough through the loop so that you can insert the end of the pencil through the buttonhole. Pull the pencil all the way through the buttonhole, and then pull the looped string tight *(Illus. D12 and D13)*.

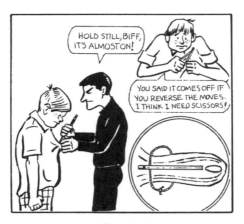

Illus. D12

Illus. D13

Once you've done this, the trick is complete. Now the spectator has to try to escape from this diabolically clever contraption. Everyone will be amused watching him trying to solve this mystery.

The solution to this problem is to simply reverse the moves that you used to fasten the pencil on the coat. Open the loop shown in *Illus. D13* and pass the eraser end of the pencil through it. When the pencil is halfway through, reach under it and take hold of the cloth by the edge of the buttonhole. Pull this cloth to the right while also pulling the pencil to the left. The pencil will come free of the loop, and you will then be able to release the loop from the buttonhole.

The Miracle Rope Trick

Here is a method for restoring a cut rope that will leave your friends truly baffled. To perform it, you will need an easily made gimmick. (A gimmick is an aid to performing a trick that your audience knows nothing about.) Cut a five-inch piece of rope from a clothesline. Make a loop of this piece and tape the ends together *(Illus. D14)*.

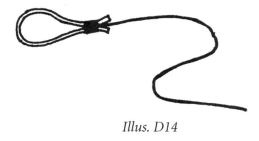

Illus. D14

Next, attach a piece of elastic cord twelve inches or more in length, depending on how long your arm is, to the taped loop. Insert the loop and elastic into the right sleeve of your suit jacket and lower it until the end of the loop is about three inches from the end of the sleeve *(Illus. D15)*.

Take a safety pin and attach the end of the elastic to the inside of your coat at the point where it enters the sleeve.

Now, put your coat on. Reach into the right sleeve with your left hand and pull the loop down into your right hand *(Illus. D16)*. When performing this trick you must keep the back of your right hand to the audience at all times.

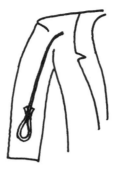

Illus. D15

To perform, walk on the stage with the loop already palmed in your right hand. With your right hand, pick up one end of a five-foot piece of clothesline from the table. With your left hand, pull the rope halfway through your right hand. Open your left hand and let the end of the rope drop.

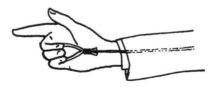

Illus. D16

Reach into your right hand and apparently pull the middle of the rope up a couple of inches so that you can cut it into two pieces with a pair of scissors. What you are actually doing is pulling the concealed loop (the gimmick) up into view *(Illus. D17)*.

Now, cut this loop with the scissors. Replace the scissors on the table. With your left hand, reach down, take the two ends of the rope, and place them in your right hand next to the two cut ends of the loop.

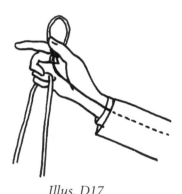

Illus. D17

Now, say the appropriate magical incantation and throw the rope towards the ceiling. The moment you open up your hand to release the rope, the cut loop will fly up your sleeve, never to be seen again. It will appear that the rope has never been cut. The movement of your arm and the speed of the elastic will effectively screen the secret of the illusion from the eyes of your audience. Another amazing trick has been performed.

A Mysterious Rope Escape

Effect: Request that two members of the audience assist you in this effect. Ask one of them to remove his jacket. Then thread 2 eight-foot lengths of rope through the arms of the jacket, and instruct the assistant to put the jacket back on and button it. The ends of both ropes should hang out of the sleeves. Take one end of rope from each sleeve and tie a single overhand knot with the ends in front of the assistant. Hand two ends of the ropes to the second assistant while retaining the other two ends in your hands. On the count of three, you and the assistant should both pull on the ropes sharply. To the amazement of all, the ropes will pass completely through the body and the coat of the first assistant.

Materials Needed:
- Two eight-foot lengths of soft nylon rope
- A short piece of white thread

Preparation: Lay the eight-foot lengths of rope out on the table and tie them together in the middle with the piece of white thread *(Illus. D18)*. Loop the thread around the ropes two or three times for strength.

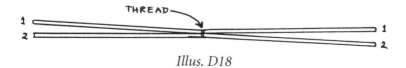

Illus. D18

Illus. D19

Illus. D20

Illus. D21

Presentation: Pick up the two pieces of rope in your right hand and show them to your audience. The middle of the ropes should be in the palm of your hand *(Illus. D19)*. Tell the audience that you are about to show them a very old rope escape that baffled Houdini. Ask two gentlemen from the audience to come forward to assist you. Make sure that one of them is wearing a jacket. Have them stand to your left, and ask the gentleman with the jacket to remove it.

While the gentleman is taking his jacket off, transfer the ropes from your right hand to your left hand. During this transfer, insert your left thumb between the ropes on one side of the white thread that holds the ropes together, and the last three fingers of your left hand between the ropes on the other side of the white thread. When you take away the rope in your left hand, the ropes will now be "linked" together by the white thread *(Illus. D20 and D21)*. In *Illus. D21*, the fingers are open to show you how this looks. During the performance keep your hand closed, with the back of it toward your audience. Practice this move so that it appears natural and you can do it without looking at your hands.

Take the jacket from the assistant and hold it up by the collar with your left hand. At all times the link that holds the ropes together must be covered by your hands. With your right hand, open up the side of the coat and ask the assistant to take the two ends of the ropes (ends 1 and 1) and push them through the sleeve of the jacket until they come out the bottom *(Illus. D22)*.

Illus. D22

Then reach over with your right hand and take the collar of the coat from your left hand, along with the ropes. Make sure that your hands cover the point where the ropes are linked together.

Next, open up the other side of the jacket with your left hand and tell the assistant to take the other two ends of the ropes (ends 2 and 2) and push them through the left sleeve until they too come out of the bottom. When this is done, step behind the assistant and help him put his jacket back on. Hold the ropes, at the collar, tightly in your hand until his arms are completely through the sleeves of the coat. This will prevent him from taking hold of the ropes in the sleeves and pulling them down, thus prematurely breaking the thread that holds them together.

Once your assistant's jacket is back on, have him button it up. Now, reach over and take one rope from each sleeve and tie them together with a single overhand knot in front of his jacket *(Illus. D23)*.

Illus. D23

Have the second assistant stand on one side of him, while you stand on the other. Hand the second assistant two ends of the ropes (ends 1 and 2); you take the other two ends in your hands. On the count of three, you should both pull sharply on the cords. The thread will break, releasing the two ropes behind the first assistant's back. The cords will slide down and out of the sleeves, and the escape will be complete.

The props for this mystery are simple; they can be examined after the trick is over, and not a clue is left to reveal the secret. This trick is amazing enough to perform in your parlor or on the stage.

A Mind-over-Matter Mystery

Effect: This trick packs the punch of a stage illusion. Your presentation goes as follows:

"My next experiment is designed to show you not how much magical power I possess, but just how much you possess. Over here on this table we have a large wooden box. The front and back panels are hinged to the sides of the box. First, I open the front panel, and then the back panel, which allows us to see completely through the box *(Illus. D24)*.

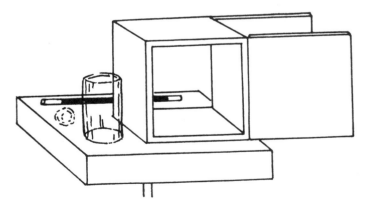

Illus. D24

"In the box, I now place this large transparent glass. On the floor of the box, next to the vase, I place this round, cotton ball (*Illus. D25*).

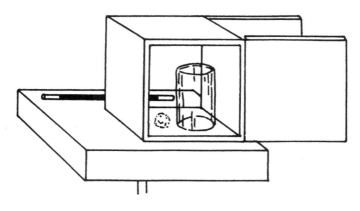

Illus. D25

"The stage is now set for you, the audience, to prove that the collective power of your minds can move mountains, or, in this case, at least one cotton ball. I want all of you, at my command, to concentrate, with all of your energies, on causing that cotton ball to rise slowly up into the air, to drift over the vase, and finally, to descend into the vase and come to rest at the bottom. Since experience has shown that this can only be done if the concentrating minds cannot see the objects involved in the experiment, I will first close and latch the back panel, and then close and latch the front panel. There, that's done.

"Now, all together, mentally command the ball to rise! Very good! Now, command it to drift over the vase! Finally, lower it gently into the vase! Very good, I think that you have done it. We will know in a moment, just as soon as I have opened the front panel. Yes, there it is, the cotton ball is resting at the bottom of the glass vase. Let me congratulate each and every one of you on a job well done."

Materials Needed:
- Wooden box
- Needle
- Black thread
- Straight-sided glass vase or tumbler
- Cotton ball
- Magic wand

Presentation: And now for the explanation. Like so many other mysterious tricks of the magician's art, the key is a piece of very fine black thread. A small hole is drilled into the top of the box.

To set up the illusion, thread a needle with the black thread and pass the needle through the hole in the top of the box. Next, pass the needle back and forth several times through the cotton ball. Form a loop on the other end of the thread and slip it over one end of the magic wand. At the moment when you place the glass vase into the box, your setup should look like the setup shown in *Illus. D26*. The black thread will, of course, be invisible to your audience.

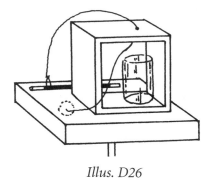

Illus. D26

When the cotton ball has been placed in the box and the doors have been closed, pick up the wand and move away from the box. When you do this, the thread attached to the wand will pull the cotton ball up inside the box until it reaches the ceiling of the box *(Illus. D27)*. The thread will then pull loose from the ball, and the ball will drop down into the vase.

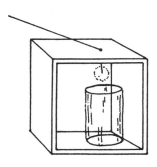

Illus. D27

Make sure that the vase is placed directly under the hole in the top of the box. Paint the inside and outside of the box black. Paint the outer rim of the box and front and back panels white. Use a glass vase that has straight sides so that the cotton ball will not snag on the way up and pull loose from the thread prematurely. The vase should also be fairly tall and wide so that the cotton ball, once it is free from the thread, will fall down into the vase, not bounce off the rim and fall outside it.

The operating principle involved with this trick is a very good one and lends itself to subtle variations. Instead of attaching the thread to the wand, the thread can extend to another room and be operated by an unseen assistant. Instead of using doors, you might drape a small cloth over the front of the box. You might do away entirely with the box and use four tall Pilsner glasses at the corners with a wicker serving tray on top and a silk cloth in front. Use your imagination, and practice well before presenting the trick.

Townsend's Ultimate Production Box

Effect: Call the audience's attention to a simple wooden box standing on a bar table. The box is sitting on a small wooden stand. Open the front door of the box and show that the interior is empty. Close the door and turn the box completely around on the stand. Still nothing to be seen. Then open both the front and the back doors of the box, allowing the audience to see completely through. Once more, close the doors and revolve the box.

The box is completely empty. Now open the top of the box and pull out a live rabbit. The Ultimate Production Box strikes again!

Materials Needed:

- Plywood
- Screws
- Glue
- Paint
- Hinges
- Mirrors
- Dowel rod
- Felt
- Hardware
- Two magnetic door catches

Construction: This is the only trick in this book that really calls for the reader to exercise his construction skills. If you're not handy around the workshop, get someone to do most or all of the woodworking, and do painting and decorating yourself. The effort that you put into constructing this production box will be amply rewarded. Although the box makes use of two old and well-known magic tricks, namely the Mirror Box and the Swing-Load Door, I have never seen both methods employed together before. You can't buy this box in the magic stores, so if you take the time to build it you'll possess a truly unique piece of equipment.

No dimensions are given with this description, as the size of the box will vary with the size of the production load. *Illus. D28* shows the box mounted on the stand with the front door open.

FRONT VIEW

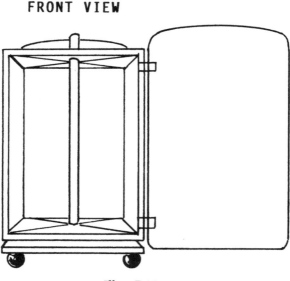

Illus. D28

The box appears empty because the load is hidden behind two mirrors in the back half of the box that are set at a 45-degree angle. The inside sides of the box are painted with vertical stripes. When viewed from the front, the mirrors give the illusion that the two sides and the back of the box are painted with stripes. The floor and the top of the inside are painted with two diagonal stripes. These stripes hide the lines of the mirrors. Running through the center of the box is a pole, which the box revolves around.

Illus. D29 shows the cabinet stand that the box sits on.

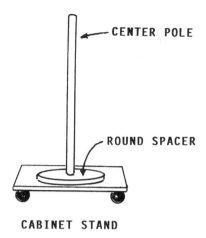

CABINET STAND

Illus. D29

The stand is raised above the table on four blocks, or feet. The floor of the stand is three-quarter-inch-thick plywood. Mounted on the center of the stand is a round three-quarter-inch-thick piece of plywood that serves as a spacer block. The top of the spacer is covered with black felt. The box sits on this felt-covered spacer, which offers little resistance when the magician is revolving the box around the stand while showing the audience that it is empty.

Through the center of the stand is a one-inch-diameter wooden dowel rod. The cabinet has holes in the center of its top and bottom, and the entire box slides down over the dowel rod when sitting on the stand.

The secret load compartment that holds the items to be produced is attached to the back door of the box. *Illus. D30* shows a view of the production box from the top when it is opened as shown in *Illus. D31.*

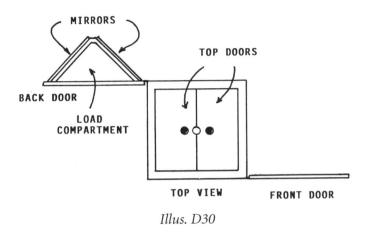

Illus. D30

The load chamber is triangular, with mirrors on its two front sides. When this door is closed, the point where the two mirrors meet is covered by the center pole of the stand. While both the front and back doors are as wide as the box, they are both longer than the height of the box. This is to prevent the audience from detecting the load chamber from the front of the box. When presenting this trick, make sure that the eye level of the audience is not above the top of the back door of the box.

Illus. D30 also shows the two doors at the top of the box. They open on either side of the center pole and have small brass knobs.

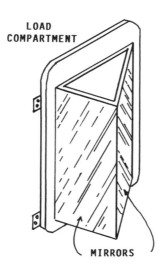

Illus. D31

Illus. D31 gives the reader a more detailed look at the load compartment on the back door.

Illus. D32 is a construction detail of the main part of the production box. It's made of three-quarter-inch-thick plywood. The boards are attached with countersunk wood screws. The holes are filled with plastic wood. Fill all holes in the edges of the plywood with plastic wood, and then sand and paint them.

Drill holes in the top and bottom boards slightly larger than the center pole of the stand. Carefully cut out the top doors, fill in their edges, and then sand and paint them. Attach the top doors with hinges to the top of the box.

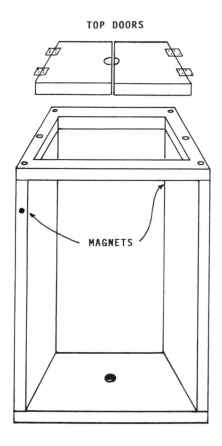

Illus. D32

Construct the front and rear doors, finish and paint them, and attach them to the box frame. The load chamber should be an eighth of an inch shorter than the inside height of the box, so that when you close the rear door it will easily slide in. This is the most delicate part of constructing the box. First, mount the rear door before attaching the load chamber to it. Close the door and, with a pencil, trace the inside of the cabinet frame onto the back door. Remove the door, place it on your workbench, and attach the load compartment to it *(Illus. D31)*. Great care should be taken in building both the load chamber and making sure that the inside of the box is perfectly square. When closed, the load chamber should fit snugly in place behind the center pole. It also should be able to move in and out of the box without binding.

Build two magnetic latches into the side frames to keep the doors from swinging open when you are turning the box around for inspection. Drill a hole into the frames about 4" from the top, and insert a round magnet so that it is flush with the outside of the wood *(Illus. D32)*. On the inside of the doors, opposite the magnets, inlay a small trip of metal. These magnetic latches will safely hold the doors shut.

When you paint the inside of the box, the two diagonal stripes on the bottom and top should be three-quarters of an inch in width. Paint all surfaces with a high-gloss enamel paint, for durability.

Presentation: By this time, the presentation of this trick should be pretty well established in your mind. *Illus. D33–Illus. D38* show how to manipulate the box.

Illus. D33 shows the box with its front door open and the load in place behind the center pole.

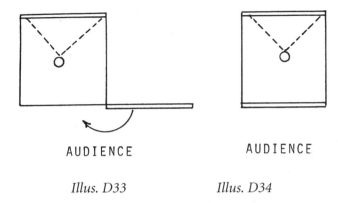

AUDIENCE

Illus. D33

AUDIENCE

Illus. D34

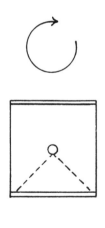

AUDIENCE

Illus. D35

Illus. D34 shows the box with its front door closed. The magician now turns the box slowly around so that the audience gets to see all sides of it.

Illus. D35 shows the box after you have finished turning it around. The back door is now facing the audience. The performer now takes hold of the back door with his right hand and the front door with his left hand and moves his hands apart. This causes the box to revolve in the direction indicated in *Illus. D35*.

Illus. D36 shows the box after it has rotated 180 degrees. The front and back doors are both open, and the load chamber is hidden behind the back door (*Illus. D33* shows the audience's view at this time). The magician gives the audience a moment to look completely through the box. He is still holding the doors in his hands as before. He now reverses his previous movements and rotates the cabinet in the opposite direction 180 degrees.

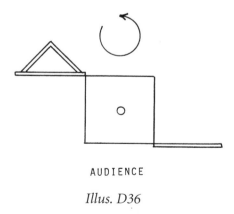

AUDIENCE

Illus. D36

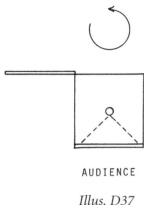

AUDIENCE

Illus. D37

Illus. D37 shows the box back at its previous position, with the back door toward the audience. The front door is still open at the back. The magician now continues to rotate the box another 180 degrees, ending up with the front of the box facing the audience and the front door still open. The audience is given a last look at the "empty" interior before the performer finally closes the door.

Illus. D38 shows the box just prior to the production of the rabbit.

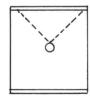

Illus. D38

The performer now reaches down and opens the two doors on the top of the box, reaches in, and pulls out the trademark of his profession…a white, furry rabbit.

Some last thoughts concerning the Ultimate Production Box: As I mentioned, there are no dimensions with the drawings given here. Construct a box to suit your production needs. If you are producing a rabbit, then the box should be just big enough to hold one. On the other hand, you may decide to produce something such as a tall, thin crystal vase half filled with water and with a red rose in it. This would call for a box of different proportions.

By this time, I think that you should understand the concept involved in using this production box. I wish you luck in your presentation of this trick. I would be interested in hearing from anyone who constructs and uses it.

The Miracle Prediction

Effect: Place a stack of business cards on the table. The stack should contain about 20 cards and be fastened with a wide rubber band. Explain that the business cards once belonged to a famous medium by the name of Voltar who passed away, and that you came across them at an estate sale last year. After reading the instructions that came with the cards, you realized that they contained a strange power that enabled Voltar to communicate from the other side. To prove this, you would like to try an experiment. Push the stack of cards forward and ask someone to write his or her initials in the rectangular box at the top of the card. Then remove this card from the stack and place it face down on the table.

Next, hand the person who initialed the card a pad of paper and request that he write down a number comprising three different digits. The number must be between one hundred and one thousand. As an example, let's say that your assistant writes down the number 732 *(Illus. D39)*.

Illus. D39

$$
\begin{array}{r}
732 \\
-237 \\
\hline
495 \\
+594 \\
\hline
1089
\end{array}
$$

He is then told to reverse the number and subtract the smaller number from the larger number. The answer in our example is 495. If the answer had been a two-digit number, your assistant would have been told to place a zero in front of it so that there will be a three-digit answer.

Finally, tell your assistant once again to reverse this number, write the reversed number below the previous answer, and then add the two numbers together. In our example the final total is 1089.

Then stretch out your hands and tell the audience that it is now time to summon the Great Voltar. Everyone is to hold hands and chant the name Voltar three times. When this is done, tell your assistant to turn over the card he initialed and see if Voltar has come through. Sure enough, when he turns it over, he will find that the number 1089 is written in red in the scroll at the bottom of the card, thus proving that there is indeed magic after death *(Illus. D40)*.

Materials Needed:
- The Voltar deck of cards as described in the Preparation section
- A pad and a pencil

Preparation: The first thing that you will need to do is to make up 40 or 50 Voltar cards. The best, and cheapest, way to do this is to take the picture of the card shown in *Illus. D41* and bring it to your local stationery store, where they can have a rubber stamp of it made up. Once you have the stamp, you can make as many cards as needed.

Illus. D40

Illus. D41

Next, you'll need several sheets of white business-card paper, which you can also get at a stationery store. After you've made up your cards, make a stack of 20 of them. Write the number 1089, in red, in the empty scroll at the bottom of the top card.

Next, take one of the cards and cut it in two. Place the bottom half of the card on top of the stack and fasten them together with a wide rubber band *(Illus. D42).* The rubber band should be at least a quarter of an inch wide. You're now ready to perform this trick.

Illus. D42

Presentation: By this time you're familiar with both the presentation of this trick and the subtle method used to reveal the answer. The number 1089 is, of course, always the right answer, no matter what three-digit number your assistant chooses. Remember, though, that the three digits that make up the number must always be different. Numbers such as 333 or 101 will not work.

The critical move in working this trick is the removal of the card from the stack in such a manner that no one sees that the number is already written on it. The bottom half of this card is covered by the half-card above *(Illus. D42).*

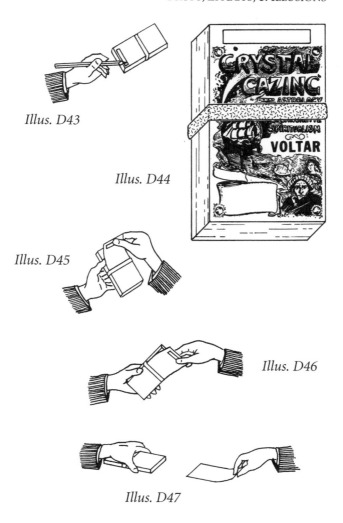

Illus. D43

Illus. D44

Illus. D45

Illus. D46

Illus. D47

When you place the stack in front of your assistant to be initialed *(Illus. D43)*, the pack does not look like it was tampered with *(Illus. D44)*. After the top card has been initialed, take hold of its top edge and bend it away from the deck *(Illus. D45)*. As you do this, start to rotate the deck away from the audience with your left hand. You should start to slide the card out from under the half-card and the rubber band with your right hand *(Illus. D46)*. Both hands continue rotating toward your side of the table until the deck, and the top card, are turned upside down and are almost touching the table. Now draw the top card completely away from the deck with your right hand and place it facedown on the table *(Illus. D47)*. This whole operation is done in one continuous movement and completely masks the card from view.

The mechanics of the trick are now complete. It's now up to you to embellish the revelation of Voltar's otherworldly powers. This is an extremely effective method of revealing things supposedly selected freely by a member of the audience.

A Mental Portrait

Effect: Step forward holding a box containing several blank slips of paper and some pencils, and say: "My next experiment deals with the science of Mental Telepathy. I would like each person in the front row to take a blank slip of paper and a pencil from this box. Just pass the box down along the row.

"Now, I want each of you to think of some famous world leader of the past and write his or her name on the slip of paper. Write any name at all, you have thousands to choose from. Watch out, don't let your neighbor see what you are writing! Are you all finished? Fine, now fold your slips and place them in the box. Very good. Will the last person who placed his slip in the box please bring it forward to me? Thank you, sir. Now, please take the box and shake it vigorously back and forth so that the slips inside will be thoroughly mixed together. I can see that you are definitely a good mixer.

"Now, when I remove the lid I want you to reach in, take out one of the slips and move over to the other side of the room. Perfect. Now, please open the slip, read the name to yourself and then concentrate on sending me a mental picture of the person whose name appears on the slip. I will, in turn, attempt to draw a picture of this person on this large sketch pad. All right, start concentrating. Yes, that's very good; I can see the figure clearly…he was an American president…he wore glasses…I see a large mustache…I see a lot of teeth…yes, it is Teddy Roosevelt…am I right? Of course I'm right, I never fail!"

Materials Needed:
- Large candy box
- Twelve or more blank pads of paper and the same number of short pencils
- Easel
- Large newsprint sketching pad

Illus. D48

Preparation: The secret to this mystery lies in the box used to collect the slips. Though it is just a large candy box, hidden in its lid is a smaller second box *(Illus. D49)*. The deep sides of the lid hide this smaller box from view.

In the beginning, remove the lid and pass out the bottom of the box, which contains the pencils and slips of paper *(Illus. D50)*. When everyone has taken a slip and a pencil, replace the lid on the box. At all times, make sure that no one is able to look inside the lid. The small box inside the lid *(Illus. D51)* is divided into two compartments.

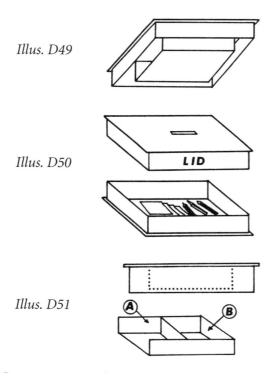

Illus. D49

Illus. D50

LID

Illus. D51

Compartment *A* is open at one end and is filled with twelve folded slips, each of which has the name of Teddy Roosevelt written on it. Compartment *B* is closed on all sides.

Presentation: Everything is done as described in the Effect section above. When the people in the front row push their folded slips into the top of the box, they all go into compartment B *(Illus. D52)*. Now, when the gentleman comes forward with the box and shakes it back and forth, all of the slips in compartment A fall to the bottom of the box *(Illus. D53)*. When he takes a slip out of the box, it has to be one with Teddy Roosevelt's name on it.

One thing that you must do when constructing the small inner box is to adhere it to the inside of the lid in such a way that you can easily remove it after every performance so that you can empty out compartment *B* and load a fresh batch of slips into compartment *A*.

You would be well advised always to use a different famous person's name each time you perform this trick so that any person witnessing it for a second time will have no clue as to your mode of operation. Practice making a rough sketch of the person whose name you are using. A few prominent features are all you will have to draw. At the conclusion of the trick, sign your masterpiece and give it to the person who assisted you as a souvenir.

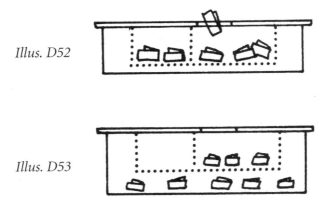

Illus. D52

Illus. D53

PLATE JUGGLING

Here are two very interesting feats of juggling that can be used as a prelude to some other trick that makes use of a plate. The first trick deals with the dropping and catching of a plate just before it hits the floor. The second feat gives the illusion of a plate rapidly revolving between your two hands. Both of these feats, or flourishes, were well documented by that most prolific of magic writers, Will Goldston, almost a century ago. Please give these tricks a try. You'll be surprised how quickly you'll become proficient at presenting them. Since I could never improve on Mr. Goldston's description of the workings of these flourishes, I'm going to turn the stage over to him.

The "Ooops!" Drop

Effect: "An amusing little piece of by-play with a plate consists in dropping it and catching it — apparently without an effort — just before it touches the ground. The trick is very showy, but it is not at all difficult to master."

Materials Needed:
- One china dinner plate
- One plastic dinner plate for practicing

Presentation: "Bend the right arm and, holding it close to the body, rest the plate on the arm, just above the cuff *(Illus. D54)*. Now, if the arm is moved downward the plate will fall, but the right hand will be exactly behind it *(Illus. D55)*. Extend the arm so that the right hand travels downwards behind the plate, the back of the hand being toward the back of the plate *(Illus. D56)*. When the plate has almost reached the ground, lift the right hand slightly, and the fingers will be in such a position that they can easily grasp the edge of the plate *(Illus. D57)*.

"The performer appears to the audience to stoop down exactly at the critical moment and to take hold of the plate just before it touches the ground; another second, apparently, and he would have been too late. The audience does not realize that the performer's hand has traveled down behind the center of the plate, and that when he wants to grasp the plate, all he has to do is the lift his right hand a few inches. In other words, what the performer does is really much easier than the feat which the audience believes he performs."

Illus. D54   *Illus. D55*   *Illus. D56*

Illus. D57

The Animated Plate

Effect: "The second feat that I'm going to explain to you deals with handling a plate in such a manner that it appears to be revolving between your hands. When the trick is done smartly, the plate seems to be running round the hands. Of course, a good deal of practice will be required before this effect is produced, and the student should practice with a plastic plate unless he is content to go through all his rehearsals while standing over a bed."

Materials Needed:
- One china dinner plate
- One plastic dinner plate for practicing

Presentation: "The directions for turning the plate must be followed very carefully, or it will be impossible to perform the feat with any certainty. The practice should be done very slowly at first, until the correct movements have been learned by heart and the student is not obliged to stop to look at the directions and the accompanying illustrations.

"The student begins by holding out his left hand with the palm uppermost and placing the plate on that hand *(Illus. D58)*.

"He then puts his right hand underneath the plate and on the side nearest to him and turns the plate by putting the little finger of the right hand against it. The plate thus turns on the left hand. When it is turned right around so that it is resting on the palm of the right hand, the left hand goes under it and turns it by raising it with the little finger. The plate thus turns on the right hand until it is brought back to the original position on the left hand, when the right hand at once begins its work once more.

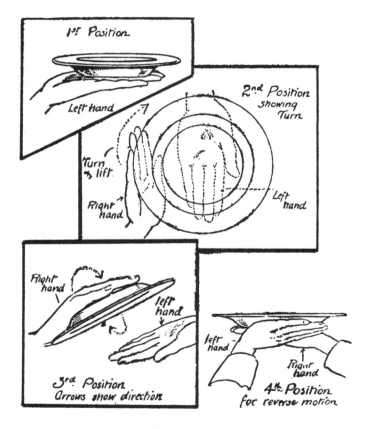

Illus. D58

"At first progress with this trick will be very slow, but with a little practice the feat will be made very effective. The great thing to remember is to raise the plate with the little fingers. The positions of the hands will seem unnatural at first, but if they are held in any other way the plate will probably fall."

SPINE-TINGLING SEANCE

The ghostly effects here were chosen for their simplicity. But even though they are easy to learn and perform, they still take practice. Practice each move over and over until you can do it without thinking.

You can find most of the materials you need to build Spooky Props around the house or in a variety of stores, and most of them don't cost much.

A Spooky Knot

Take out a pocket handkerchief and let it hang from the fingertips of your right hand.

Say, "You can always tell when there's a ghost around. They like to play pranks. They like to tie knots in things without your knowing about it. I'll show you what I mean."

Lift the corner of the handkerchief with your left hand and hold it with your right fingertips. Shake it out with a snap. No knot appears. Say, "I guess there's no ghost around here."

Try it again. Still no knot. Say, "Maybe he's just shy. Maybe if we ask him nicely, he'll come out."

Shake the handkerchief loose one more time. This time, to everyone's surprise, there is suddenly a knot tied in the end of the handkerchief. This is an easy, but very effective illusion.

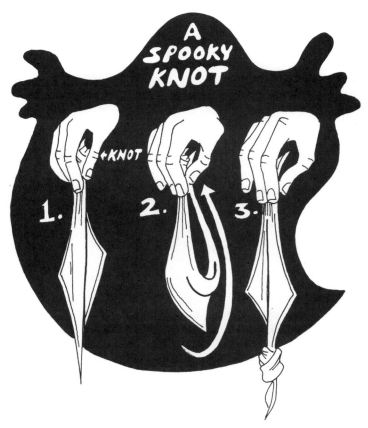

Illus. D59

Begin by tying a knot in the corner of a handkerchief. Hold the end with the knot in your right hand so it is hidden by your fingers (1).

Gather the other end of the handkerchief in your hand (2). The first two times you shake out the handkerchief, release the end without the knot. The last time you shake it out, release the end with the knot (3).

It will look to your audience as if a knot appeared in the handkerchief from nowhere.

The Spirited Handkerchief

Show a handkerchief with a knot tied on one of its ends and then drape it over the palm of your right hand.

Say, "Ghosts tie knots in things because they like to hide in there and use the object — like the bodies they no longer have."

Suddenly, the knotted end of the handkerchief stands straight up, quivers for a moment, then falls back down.

Say, "There's a ghost in here all right. We have to be careful. Once they show themselves, sometimes they try to get away."

The handkerchief stands upright abruptly, then seems to try to fly out of your hand. You have to catch it with your left hand to keep it from getting away.

Say: "He was trying to fly away. He must be in high spirits."

"The Spirited Handkerchief" isn't as ordinary as it appears. In order to make it work, push a short piece of wire under the hem of the handkerchief against the knot.

WIRE IN HEM ↗

Illus. D60

To make it rise and fall, push against the edge of the hidden wire with your thumb.

To make it try to fly away, simply extend your hand as if the handkerchief were flying away and you were just hanging on to it. Reach out and grab the knot with your other hand.

Drape it over the other hand to make it rise again.

The Phantom Tube

A plain, white pocket handkerchief rests on a table beside a metal tube (a tin can) sealed on both ends with plastic lids. Pick up the handkerchief and wad it into a ball.

Say: "Ghosts like to hide in handkerchiefs so you won't know what they really look like."

Pick up the tube and remove the lid on top. Show that it's empty. Put the handkerchief inside and replace the lid. Set the can back on the table.

Say: "Sometimes, if they like you, the ghosts will show themselves as they really are."

Pick up the tube and remove the lid again. Reach inside.

Instead of a white handkerchief, there's a white ghost in there with a round head and two, empty black eyes!

The secret is in the tube, which has a false bottom in the middle painted black, and two identical lids on the ends.

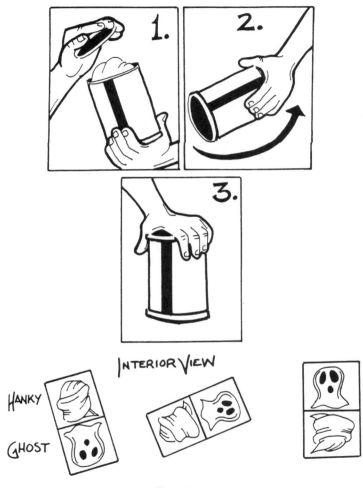

Illus. D61

Materials:
- Empty 24-ounce juice can (.7 liter juice tin)
- Piece of stiff cardboard
- 2 identically colored plastic lids
- Flat black paint
- White glue

Clean the tin can and remove the label. Use a can opener to remove both ends of the can. Using one of the can tops — (be careful — its edges are sharp!) — trace a circle on the cardboard and cut it out with a scissors as in *Illus. D62*.

Push the cardboard circle into the center of the tin can. It should fit snugly. Put a bead of white glue around the outside of both sides of the cardboard circle (*Illus. D62*).

Once the glue has dried, paint the inside of both chambers of the can flat black. This way the cardboard in the center of the can will not reflect any light, making it impossible to tell how deep the can really is.

Fix the plastic lids on the ends of the can, and there you have it.

The small ghost (described in the next trick, *The Floating Ghost*) is inside the lower section of the tube before the trick begins.

When you open the upper part, it appears to be an ordinary, metal tube. Holding the tube on the palm of your left hand, you place the handkerchief inside the upper compartment. Turn your left hand over as in *Illus. D61*, turning the tube over as well, and place it on the table. Now the compartment containing the ghost is on top.

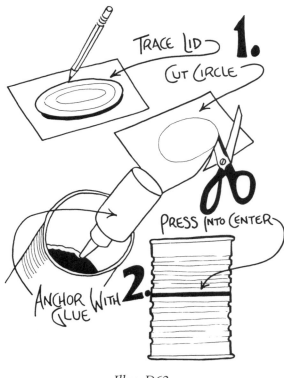

TRACE LID **1.**
CUT CIRCLE
PRESS INTO CENTER
ANCHOR WITH **2.**
GLUE

Illus. D62

Pick up the tube again, remove the lid and pull out the ghost. Turn the tube toward the audience and show it is now empty.

People will think they've seen a hanky become a ghost before their very eyes.

The Floating Ghost

Hold a small, round-headed "ghost" with black eyes and moaning mouth directly in front of you between the fingers of both hands.

Say: "This little spook is a friend. He'll float in the air just for me."

Slowly draw your fingers away. The ghost floats in midair between your extended palms. It tries to fly away. Catch it in midair. It continues to float up and down at your command. The secret of the floating ghost is a combination of puppetry and prestidigitation.

The floating ghost has a hole in the back of its head just big enough for the tip of your thumb to fit inside. Since your thumb is hidden behind the ghost, it appears as if the ghost is floating between your hands (*Illus. D63*).

Illus. D63

Make it rise and fall by moving both hands alongside. Make it seem to fly away by quickly extending both hands and then "clutching" the ghost with your fingertips. Switch the hand that puts its thumb in the back of the ghost and make it float again. This will reduce suspicion about what's *really* happening.

Practice in front of a mirror until the "floating" action appears mysterious, but natural.

Materials:
- 2-inch (5cm) Styrofoam ball
- 18-inch (45cm) white handkerchief or scarf
- Small piece of black felt
- Straight pins
- White glue

Press your thumb into the ball to make a hole or depression deep enough so that the ball will stay on your thumb during the performance (1).

Next, take a pair of scissors and make a single cut up the middle edge of the scarf to just below the center (2).

Drape the scarf over the ball with the cut over the hole (3).

Secure the scarf to the ball with straight pins.

Cut eyes and a mouth from the black felt, and glue them to the front of the ghost (4).

Note: Use a silk or rayon scarf for the shroud of "The Floating Ghost" if you intend to use the ghost in "The Phantom Tube." Silk or rayon is much less bulky than cotton or other material.

If you don't intend to use "The Floating Ghost" with "The Phantom Tube," an ordinary white handkerchief is fine for the shroud.

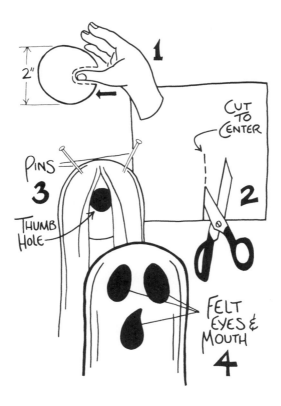

Illus. D64

Apparition in the Dark

The lights go out. The room is dark. Suddenly the glowing figure of a ghost appears from nowhere and begins to dance in the gloom. Just as suddenly, it disappears into thin air.

Where did it come from? Where did it go?

It came from your pocket, and that's where it went, too.

Take a piece of heavy black material about 2 x 4 feet (60cm x 1.2m) and paint the picture of a ghost on it with glow-in-the-dark paint.

Make a hem along the top of the material and slip two 12-inch-long (30cm) sticks inside.

Expose the picture to a very bright light for a few hours before you are going to use it.

Fold the picture in half, roll it up and conceal it. To make the ghost appear, suddenly turn out the lights, unroll the picture and open it up. The ghost will seem to appear from nowhere.

Move the top of it up and down. The ghost will appear to dance. Close it up, and the ghost disappears.

Note: Glow-in-the-dark, or luminous, paint is readily available at most craft stores.

The Vanishing and Reappearing Wand

Open a plain, business-size envelope and take a black magic wand with white tips from inside it. Put the envelope on the table. Say, "This magic wand belongs to the spirit of an old wizard. If we can hide it from him, it may give us spooky magic too."

Place the wand on a piece of newspaper and roll it inside. Say, "I don't think the wizard will let us keep it, though." Crumple the rolled newspaper tube and toss it over your shoulder. Say, "I didn't think so."

Open the envelope on the table. The wand is back inside.

Materials:
- Short piece of dowel
- Black paint
- White paint
- Black construction paper
- Envelope

To prepare for this trick, make a magic wand by taking the short piece of dowel and painting it black with white tips.

Next, take a piece of black construction paper and roll the wand in it. Tape it tightly. Paint the tips of this construction paper tube white so it looks like the wand (1). Put the wand inside the tube, and place both inside the envelope.

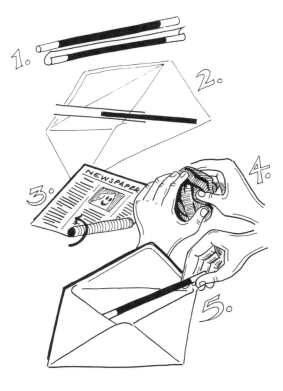

Illus. D65

When you open the envelope, take the paper tube wand out, but let the real wand remain in the envelope (2). Wrap the paper tube in the newspaper (3).

When you wad the newspaper (4), you're wadding the paper wand as well.

Take the real wand out of the envelope (5).

It will seem to have vanished from the newspaper and re-appeared in the envelope. Let everyone inspect the wand and the envelope if they want to.

Wand Through the Hanky

Pick up an ordinary handkerchief and show it on both sides. Say, "In a really haunted place, nothing is as solid as it looks."

Drape the handkerchief over your left fist and poke your right thumb into the center to make a small pocket. Take a short black magic wand with white tips (an ordinary pencil or pen will do) and stick it into the pocket in the center of the hanky.

Say, "This wand wouldn't be able to pass through the hanky in my hand unless the place were haunted."

Have a member of the audience push down on the top of the wand. At first it resists. Pass your right hand over the top of the wand a couple of times and then ask the spectator to push down on it again. This time it seems to slowly melt through the handkerchief.

Pull it free from the bottom. Show the handkerchief again to prove there is no hole in it.

The secret of this trick lies in the way you make the pocket in the center of the handkerchief with your thumb.

Illus. D66

To the audience, it looks as if you're poking your thumb straight down in the center of the handkerchief. What actually happens is that when your thumb presses downward, the forefinger and thumb of your left hand underneath the handkerchief separate so that (1) the outside of the handkerchief is pressed against the inside of your left hand (2) your left forefinger and thumb pinch the hanky around your right thumb.

When you withdraw your thumb, it looks as if a pocket or depression has been left. Push the wand into the depression (3), but hold the little finger of your left hand (under the hanky) below it to keep it in place. Slowly release the pressure of your little finger. The wand will seem to melt through the handkerchief (4).

The Penetrating Key

Take an ordinary house key from your pocket and hold it up between the thumb and forefinger of your left hand.

Say, "Have you ever reached into your pocket and realized you lost your key? That's probably because a spook stole it. They can make keys go right through your clothes, and as you know, they love to play tricks on people."

Cover your left hand, along with the keys with a pocket handkerchief. Lift a corner of the handkerchief to show the audience that the key is underneath. Flip the handkerchief back over it and then twist it around the key. To everyone's amazement, the key will come right through the center of the handkerchief!

Let it fall free into the palm of your right hand, and then show the handkerchief to prove there isn't a hole in it. There really isn't a hole in the center of the handkerchief, although that's what it really does look like to the audience.

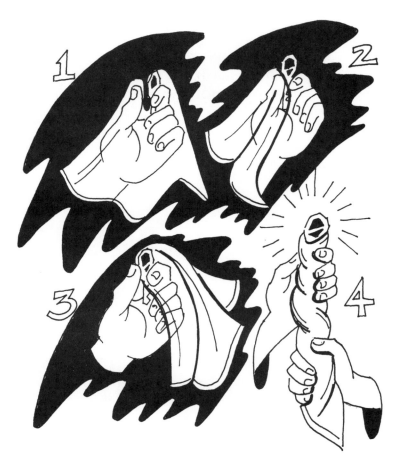

Illus. D67

Here's how it works:

Hold the key up between your right forefinger and thumb. Cover it with the hanky. Pinch the hanky between the edge of the key and your right thumb once it's covered (1).

After you flip the handkerchief back to show the audience that the key really is in the center (2), the key will appear to be inside the fold—but since you've flipped the entire handkerchief forward, it's really hidden behind the hanky and is held in place by your thumb (3).

Twist the handkerchief until the key appears and falls from the top into the open palm of your right hand (4).

Tumbler Through Tumbler

Show two identical plastic tumblers. Say, "You may think the idea of ghosts is one that doesn't hold water, but I can prove that you're wrong."

Pick up the tumblers in both hands and hold one over the other. Say, "When the spirits are around, nothing holds anything."

Drop the top tumbler into the bottom tumbler. Everyone will be stunned as it melts right through and falls to the table!

Just to prove that the tumbler is really immaterial, hold it by the fingertips of your left hand. Hold an identical tumbler over the top of it in your right hand.

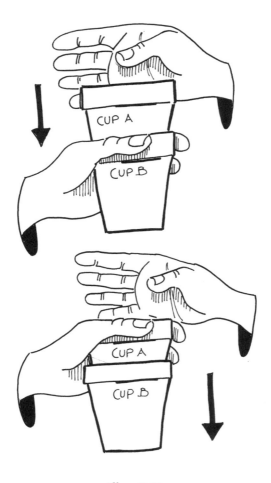

Illus. D68

Drop the top tumbler into the bottom one. At the same time, release your grip on the bottom tumbler and catch the rim of the top one.

To your audience, it looks as if the top tumbler has fallen through the bottom one—proof positive that the tumbler is as immaterial as a ghost!

Remember, this is a quick effect, so dropping and catching the tumblers has to be perfectly timed to make it work.

The Noisy Poltergeist

Assemble a number of small items on a table including a small metal bell, a deck of playing cards, a wand or a pencil and a couple different-colored balls. Hold a large handkerchief or a table napkin about 18 inches (45cm) square by the upper corners.

Say, "Poltergeists are noisy, and they like to throw things around. But they don't like to be seen because they're shy. You have to give them some privacy before they'll do their work."

Show both sides of the napkin, then hold it in front of the items on the table. Suddenly, cards start flying over the top of the napkin into the audience, followed by the balls. The bells begin mysteriously ringing. The pencil pokes over the top of the napkin. Then it flies over the top followed by the bell.

Pull the napkin away. There's absolutely nothing there.

Bend a pin into a hook and stick it into the left corner of the napkin. Show the front side of the napkin (1). Show the reverse side of the napkin by drawing the left corner toward your right shoulder while swinging your right arm in front of your left arm (2). Turn your body slightly to the left, and drape the napkin in front of the objects on the table so they are hidden from the audience.

Illus. D69

Pin the corner of the napkin just below your armpit, holding it in place. This leaves your left hand free behind the napkin to toss objects over the top of it, ring the bell and so forth (3).

INTERIOR VIEW

Illus. D70

Your audience however won't know this. With a little practice, you'll make it look as if your left hand is really holding a corner of the napkin just as your right one is.

The Rising Cards

Take out a deck of playing cards and, while shuffling them, say, "Ghosts and goblins love card tricks. And I have an invisible ghost who will help me do this one."

Have someone from the audience choose a card, show it to the rest of the audience and place it on top of the deck. Cut the cards and hold them vertically in your left hand with their faces toward the audience.

Say, "I didn't see which card you chose, but I don't have to. My ghostly friend will find it for me." Place your right index finger on the top of the deck. Slowly raise your right hand. The card that was chosen by the audience member slowly rises out of the pack with it!

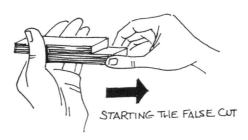

STARTING THE FALSE CUT

Illus. D71

The secret to this trick is to make certain the chosen card remains on the top of the deck. Do this by using a move called "the false cut."

To work the false cut, hold the deck along the edges face down between the thumb and fingers of your left hand. Grasp the *bottom* portion of the deck with your right hand, as the illustration shows, and cut away the bottom portion of cards.

Tap them against the edge of the cards in your left hand. Then carry them over the top and place them on the table. Take the rest of the cards from your left hand and drop them on top of the cards on the table with your right hand.

This looks like a regular, innocent cut. But actually, you've re-assembled the deck exactly as it was to begin with. The chosen card is still face down on the top of the deck.

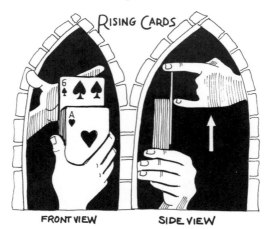

FRONT VIEW   SIDE VIEW

Illus. D72

Place the deck between the thumb and fingers of your left hand with the faces of the cards toward the audience. Hold it in front of you with the top of the deck tilted slightly toward your body.

As you place your right forefinger on top of the deck, extend your little finger behind the deck so it touches the back of the chosen card. As you lift your right hand, your little finger pushes the chosen card upwards. As far as your audience is concerned, an invisible ghost is making it rise.

The Tell-Tale Timepiece

Pull out a scroll and unroll it on a table. On the scroll is the picture of a clock. Say, "Ghosts are restless, but they are always on time. They are going to appear at an exact hour."

Arbitrarily point to someone. Say, "The spirits will tell you exactly when." Ask that person to merely *think* of an hour pictured on the clock. Pick up a pencil. Say you are going to tap the pencil point on the numbers of the clock. Tell your volunteer to count as you tap, starting with the number he thought of and adding one to that number.

For example, if your subject chooses the number seven on the clock, he will add one to the number and mentally count "eight" the first time the pencil point hits the clock. He'll then count "nine," "ten," and so forth. Tell him to say "Stop" when he *mentally* reaches 20. He, and everyone else watching, will be amazed when your pencil point is on the hour the volunteer thought of the instant he cries "Stop!"

Sound impossible? The ghosts say boo to that! All you have to do is remember the number seven. When you start tapping, tap the pencil point at random all over the clock until you reach seven. After reaching the number seven—on the eighth tap—place the pencil point on 12, and continue tapping counter-clockwise until the volunteer says, "Stop."

If your volunteer can count—and is honest—your pencil point will rest on the hour he chose every time.

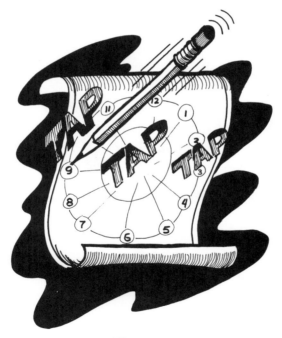

Illus. D73

The Killer Tomato

Set two tin cans with both of their ends removed beside each other on a tabletop. One is an 8-ounce tomato sauce can, the other is a 16-ounce tomato soup tin or whole-tomato can.

Say, "Some of the strangest movie monsters of all time were the Killer Tomatoes. Killer Tomatoes would jump off vines and roll out of the supermarket. Sometimes they'd come right out of the can to get you!"

Pick up the larger of the two twin cans and show that it's empty. Drop the smaller through it to prove the point, then show that the small one is empty too. Drop the smaller tin through the larger one again, and hold the smaller one in the palm of your hand.

Say, "Just because these tin cans are empty, it doesn't mean we're safe. Killer tomatoes are like ghosts. You never know where they'll show up."

Pluck the tin can from your palm. There's a killer tomato resting on it!

Quickly toss it into the audience and watch them jump.

Materials:
- 8-ounce (240ml) tomato sauce can
- 16-ounce (.47 liter) tomato soup tin or whole-tomato can
- Plastic tomato
- Hook

Preparation: To produce "The Killer Tomato," fix a hook into a plastic tomato just big enough to fit inside the small tin can. Place the tomato inside with the hook on the upper edge (1) prior to showing the trick.

Illus. D74

When you drop the small tin can through the larger one, the hook on the tomato will catch on the upper edge of the large can (2). Once the small tin can has fallen through the larger one, turn the larger one over in the palm of your hand so that the tomato is now on your palm.

Drop the small tin through the larger one again (3), and lift it up and away, leaving the small can and the tomato on your palm. When you remove the smaller can, the tomato will seem to have appeared out of nowhere!

INDEX